SPLENDORS
OF THE
ROSARY

Publisher: Pierre-Marie Dumont
Editor: Romain Lizé
Assistants to the editor: Thérèse de Cathelineau, Pascale van de Walle, Emmanuelle Lebrun

Meditations and art commentaries: Pierre-Marie Dumont
Research for art commentaries: Christine Charier
Commentaries on flowers: Thérèse de Cathelineau / Pierre-Marie Dumont
Editor for hymns: Jeremy Schwager
Translation: Janet Chevrier
Copyediting: Andrew Matt and Susan Needham

Art Direction: Elisabeth Hébert
Layout: Élise Borel
Iconography: Isabelle Mascaras
Production: Sabine Marioni
Photo engraving: Point4

ISBN: 978-1-936260-44-7
First edition: October 2012

www.magnificat.com

Pierre-Marie Dumont

SPLENDORS
OF THE
ROSARY

MAGNIFICAT

Paris • New York • Oxford • Madrid

TABLE OF CONTENTS

How Magnificent
Is the History of the Rosary!

Bishop Jacques Perrier
Former Bishop of Lourdes

It is beautiful to see how generations of Christians, from the Gospel on, have created their prayers.

As early as the second or third century, a graffito in Nazareth contained an abbreviated form of the first two words of the angelic greeting, but with one difference. In the Gospel according to Saint Luke, the angel addresses Mary, but does not call her by her name. In a masterpiece of grace, he addresses her as "full of grace." When praying to her, Christians used the name her parents gave her, the name Saint Joseph surely used when speaking to his wife: "Mary." Christians adopted the words of the angel and made of them their prayer.

To the angel's greeting, Christians joined Elizabeth's blessing. "Rejoice," the angel had said. "Blessed art thou," added Elizabeth. Joy and blessing— the two fundamental themes of the Gospel.

All Prayer Rises
to the Father

Some time later, an intercession was added. Mary was proclaimed "Holy" and the "Mother of God," according to the faith as defined at the Third Ecumenical Council held in Ephesus in 431. As she is at one and the same time Mother of God and our Mother, she is particularly well placed to present our petitions to him who alone can grant them, and at two decisive moments, the present and the final moment: now and at the hour of our death. She intercedes for us as she did at Cana: "They have no more wine."

But the rosary is not just a series of Hail Marys. Every set of ten beads, or decade, begins with the Our Father that Jesus taught us to pray, and ends with the acclamation of the Trinity: *Glory to the Father, and to the Son, and to the Holy Spirit...* We enter into the rosary with a sign of the cross and the Creed. It is because the prayer of the rosary is not directed toward herself that it is authentically Marian: "The Mighty One has done great things for me, and holy is his name." "Hallowed be thy name," we say in the Our Father. Even from the cross, Jesus "revealed" the name of the Father, as he says in his Priestly Prayer.

The first Our Father reminds us that ultimately all prayer must rise to the Father, the source of all life and all holiness. The three Hail Marys preceding the first decade recall the Trinity and the three virtues of faith, hope, and charity. These are called the "theological" virtues because they come to us from God and are about God in whom we place all our faith, our hope, and our love.

Thus the prayer of the rosary has gradually evolved. It does not consist in the mechanical repetition of multiple Hail Marys. Even the number of one hundred and fifty is not without significance, since it corresponds to the number of psalms recited by monks and priests throughout the week. In this, the rosary is linked to the official prayer of the Church, to liturgical prayer.

The rosary has matured in various times and places, but it is the Dominican Order that has been its most ardent promoter. It existed before Saint Dominic or Saint Catherine of Siena, but these two saints are indissociable from it.

CONTEMPLATING CHRIST WITH HIS MOTHER

Over the course of the centuries, the rosary was further enriched by the meditation upon the mysteries of Christ. Each set of ten beads corresponds to moments in the life of Christ, from his Incarnation to his glorification. A mystery is not an enigma but a reality charged with meaning and life. Because he is the eternal Word and because he is risen, each moment in the life of Christ, each "mystery," is not simply something in the past. Jesus was born under Herod the Great; he died and rose again under Pontius Pilate: this happened once and for all in the past. But these events still remain sources of grace. This is why we celebrate them in the liturgy. At Christmas Mass, we say: "Today a great light has shone upon the earth." In God, nothing is ever past or surpassed.

All popes of recent centuries have written about the rosary. Leo XIII published numerous encyclicals on the subject. Blessed John Paul II was the most bold of all. At the end of the Great Jubilee of 2000, he asked the Church to "start again from Christ" and to become above all a "school of prayer." Two years later in 2002, in an Apostolic Letter on the rosary, he wrote that reciting the rosary is a school of popular prayer where we learn to contemplate Christ in the company of Mary, his mother and our Mother.

This letter gives very useful advice for the fruitful praying of the rosary, which John Paul II said was his favorite prayer. Before him, the rosary was composed of three cycles of mysteries: the joyous, the sorrowful, and the glorious. Pope John Paul II had no hesitation in adding the luminous mysteries, taken from the years of Jesus' public ministry. He wished in this way to accentuate the Christological character of the rosary. He had learned from Saint Louis-Marie Grignion de Montfort that true devotion to Mary — *Totus tuus* — is devotion to Christ. The pope wished it to be clear that, in reciting the rosary, it is the person of Christ who has primacy of place.

The pope's boldness was twofold. First, he added a series of mysteries, feeling unconstrained by the number of one hundred and fifty, despite the long tradition. And then, he made a proposal to the Church in a domain that was not strictly within his authority, given that the rosary is not a liturgical prayer like those of the sacraments or of the divine office. The pope acted in the role of a spiritual father seeking to help those who trusted in him along the path of faith.

ENTER INTO THE SPLENDORS OF THE ROSARY

The Catholic world has embraced these luminous mysteries. On the other hand, many of the pope's other recommendations were not put into practice. One of them concerns the meditation upon the Gospel which should accompany the praying of the rosary: the following pages are an example of this. The artwork illustrates these splendors of the rosary. But the history of the rosary itself is magnificent — it demonstrates how the Holy Spirit enriches the spiritual legacy of the Church.

In Lourdes, the Virgin gave Bernadette a prayer that was for her alone. What a privilege! Bernadette never revealed its contents. She said it every day. And yet, each day, she also said the rosary. And when she prayed the rosary, she became almost as beautiful as she was during the apparitions of the Virgin. What an encouragement to us!

Joyful Mysteries

"To meditate upon the 'joyful' mysteries, then,
is to enter into the ultimate causes
and the deepest meaning of Christian joy.
It is to focus on the realism
of the mystery of the Incarnation
and on the obscure foreshadowing
of the mystery of the saving Passion."

Blessed John Paul II
Rosarium Virginis Mariae 20

The Marian symbolism of the lily is implicit in, among other places, a verse from the Song of Songs: "As a lily among thorns, so is my beloved among women" (Sgs 2:2). Considered by the Greeks "the flower of flowers," it is only natural that the lily should accompany the Virgin, the most beautiful flower of paradise. For this reason, it has been named the "madonna lily."

Through its brilliant whiteness, the lily symbolizes purity, virginity, and chastity. Traditionally held by the angel Gabriel in depictions of the Annunciation, it is also the attribute of Saint Joseph. As early as the eleventh century, Mary was represented with a lily on coins minted by bishops. The perfume of the lily is also associated with the odor of sanctity.

THE VIRGIN

Mother! Whose virgin bosom was uncrost
With the least shade of thought to sin allied;
Woman! Above all women glorified,
Our tainted nature's solitary boast;
Purer than foam on central ocean tost;
Brighter than eastern skies at daybreak strewn
With fancied roses, than the unblemished moon
Before her wane begins on heaven's blue coast.

The First Joyful Mystery
THE ANNUNCIATION

Most blessed are you among women,
for the Father of the ages chose you,
Virgin Mary, daughter of Zion,
that the Word spoken to you
might become flesh in your womb.

The "yes" of Mary, daughter of Zion, is pure and simple,[1] unencumbered by any ifs, ands, or buts. Sarah laughs when the Lord promises her a son;[2] Zechariah has serious doubts too.[3] But Mary believes. And yet it is even more improbable that she should be chosen from among all women to become the mother of the Messiah than that they might bear children in old age!

Like all of us sinners, Sarah and Zechariah first consider the difficulties from the human perspective, unable to see beyond the rational improbability of the fulfillment of the divine promise. But Mary places her faith in God, whom she knows to be *merciful* and *abounding in love*.[4] She is unafraid before him for whom nothing is impossible.[5] And yet, she is not above the need to satisfy her intellect. "How can this be?" she quite naturally asks the angel.[6] His response demonstrates the extent to which God respects the queries of the rational mind he created. Faith itself generates the questions to which God's answers, in turn, provoke a further deepening of faith.

Through contemplation of the mystery of the Incarnation of Christ, let us ask Mary to teach us the simplicity of her beautiful faith—the pure faith of true sons and daughters of Abraham, a faith unobscured by incredulity, skepticism, or fear of the future—the luminous faith of the *Theotokos*, the chosen Mother of God.

1- *Lk 1:58*   2- *Gn 18:12*   3- *Lk 1:20*
4- *Ps 145:8*   5- *Lk 1:37*   6- *Lk 1:34*

Prayer

God our Father, who willed that at the angel's Annunciation
your Word be made flesh in the womb of the Virgin Mary,
we beseech you to answer our entreaties.
As we truly believe her to be the Mother of God,
may our Lady's prayers to you bring us your aid.
Through Christ our Lord.

The Virgin of the Annunciation (after 1440)
Stefan Lochner (c. 1410-1451), oil on wood, 102.8 x 55.9 in.
Exterior panel of the Altarpiece of the Three Kings, Germany, Cologne Cathedral, Germany

In an interior hung with brocades, a very young girl, a wonder of delicacy and reserve, is surprised in splendid humility as she kneels in prayer before a book of the psalms. The painter has captured this "most blessed among women" at that singular instant when, the angel having told her, "The Holy Spirit will come upon you, and the power of the Most High will overshadow you," she responds, "May it be done to me according to your word." At her feet, the book of the Old Testament lies henceforth closed, symbolizing the veiled presence of the Word of God already sown in the heart of this daughter of Zion. In this moment chosen by the artist, time seems suspended before the immensity of this event, before the book of the new covenant is opened, before the unimaginable takes place, before the Word begotten, not made, takes on a body and a face in the womb of this daughter of Eve. He will be the new Adam. In the new creation, he will transform sin into grace. In this apocalyptic instant when the Eternal comes to inhabit the temporal, Lochner invites us to pause and contemplate this woman as she was when she came forth from God in the morning of her original splendor.

The dahlia, symbol of gratitude, refers directly to the *Magnificat*, the Virgin Mary's canticle of thanksgiving to God. In this bouquet, the reference is further heightened by the brilliant red and orange colors of the nasturtiums, also called "capucines" because their shape is similar to a monk's cowl. Charmed by the nasturtium's decorative as well as comestible qualities, King Louis XIV introduces it to France to enhance the dishes served at the royal table. Since then, in the language of flowers, it signifies sentiments of exaltation. It thus serves as a most apt evocation of the words of the canticle that flowed from the heart of Mary at the Visitation: "My soul proclaims the greatness of the Lord; my spirit rejoices in God my savior" (Lk 1:47).

AVE MARIA

Ave Maria, gratia plena,	Hail Mary, full of grace.
Dominus tecum,	The Lord is with thee.
benedicta tu in mulieribus,	Blessed art thou among women,
et benedictus	and blessed is the fruit of thy womb,
fructus ventris tui Jesus.	Jesus.
Sancta Maria mater Dei,	Holy Mary, Mother of God,
ora pro nobis peccatoribus,	pray for us sinners,
nunc, et in hora mortis nostrae.	now and at the hour of our death.
Amen.	Amen.

The Second Joyful Mystery
THE VISITATION

Blessed be the Lord, the God of Israel;
for he has come to his people and set them free.
He has raised up for us a mighty Savior,
born of the house of his servant David.
Through his holy prophets he promised of old
that he would save us.

By leaving *in haste* to visit her cousin Elizabeth,[1] the Virgin Mary demonstrates her eagerness to share the saving mystery of God who "has visited and brought redemption to his people."[2] She is thus a figure of the Church who, strengthened by the sacraments and filled with the Holy Spirit, visits all people to make known Christ the Savior. She is also a model for all Christians who, having received the Body of Christ, bear within themselves the fruit of salvation—not to be savored closed within themselves, but rather *in haste* to communicate its joy and charity to all people on earth.

The Father first surrounds us with the members of our family, as well as all those he places along our path through life. He wishes us to be a true sign of his love to each one of them. Our own personal vocation is most often fulfilled through a loving openness to those close to us. Such was the openness of Mary to her cousin Elizabeth, as well as, later, to her neighbors in Nazareth. It is this same vocation to which Jesus specifically calls the paralytic[3] and the Gerasene after he heals them: "Go home to your family and announce to them all that the Lord in his pity has done for you."[4] In our homes, within our families, in a triumph of humility, may our hearts be open to this shared joy and our lives become a hymn of exultation to the glory of God.

Through contemplation of the mystery of the Visitation, let us learn from Mary her haste to brotherly service and the blessedness of sharing. By her example, may we show ourselves worthy, through the holiness of our lives, to transmit the joy of salvation to our brothers and sisters.

1- *Lk 1:39* 2- *Lk 1:68* 3- *Mk 2:11* 4- *Mk 5:19*

Prayer

God, our Father,
by the arrival of the Virgin Mary, carrying our Savior within her,
you brought salvation and joy to the house of Elizabeth.
Teach us to follow the inspiration of the Holy Spirit
that we too may know how to bear Christ to our brothers and sisters
and to magnify your name through hymns and the holiness of our lives.
Through Christ our Lord.

The Visitation (c. 1610-1614)
Domenikos Theotokopoulos, called El Greco (1541-1614), oil on wood, 38 x 28.1 in.

In this Visitation, El Greco daringly places Mary on the same footing as her cousin Elizabeth, distinguishing them by neither size nor position nor pose—not even in the color of their garments. But a few edges of Mary's fire-red gown are visible: for beneath the cloak of her humanity, Mary is clothed with the Holy Spirit. This Visitation is a meditation on the intimate mystery of a hidden presence who has come to visit a soul plunged in the night, making her thrill with joy. The mystical God of the righteous is not a god of the imagination or dreams: he is God incarnate, a God hidden within the womb of his own humanity, just as he was hidden in the womb of Mary at the time of the Visitation. El Greco asks us here to learn from Elizabeth and John the Baptist how to discern him within the depths of our own dark night, when, borne by Mary, he comes to visit us.

Inspired by his own intense spiritual journey, El Greco, a quintessentially Spanish and Catholic painter, divests his artwork of all artifice: nothing remains but the elevation of earth to heaven, the rhythm of light and shadow. The decor is stylized in the extreme, the hands and faces reduced to their essence. It is as though the exaltation of the subjects is sublimated into the rendering of the tragic vestments that almost entirely engulf them. The artist who refused to go out in the noonday sun, saying, "The glare of daylight would spoil my inner light," has clothed Mary and her cousin Elizabeth in swathes of an apocalyptic sky, that of the darkness which came over the whole land on Good Friday from noon until three in the afternoon (Lk 23:44). The outline of their cloaks is etched by the play of bursts of light ripping through a storm-darkened sky. But the black sky is transfigured by the flashes of that electric-blue which so fascinated Picasso: as with Saint John of the Cross, the shadows of this dark night are given all their meaning when sculpted by a brilliant flame of love.

The daylily is the emblem of maternity. In Christian art, it is commonly associated with the Nativity of the Lord, as for example in the famous *Portinari Triptych* by Hugo Van der Goes (Uffizi Galleries, Florence). Often equated with the lily, which has the same shape, the daylily recalls Mary's virginity, while its orange hue suggests the union between God and man, thus symbolizing the Mystical Marriage. It is a perfectly apt choice to honor Mary, who became the Mother of God without loss of the glory of her virginity.

The presence of red petunias is suggestive of a bloody accident, while, in the language of flowers, violet petunias express great vulnerability. These flowers are always associated with a tragic event. Their inclusion in this bouquet is in strong contrast to the joy of Christmas: they foreshadow the massacre of the Holy Innocents as well as the cross destined for the holy newborn Infant.

A CHRISTMAS CAROL

In the bleak mid-winter
Frosty wind made moan,
Earth stood hard as iron,
Water like a stone;
Snow has fallen, snow on snow,
Snow on snow,
In the bleak mid-winter
Long ago.

Our God, Heaven cannot hold Him
Nor earth sustain;
Heaven and earth shall flee away
When He comes to reign:
In the bleak mid-winter
A stable-place sufficed
The Lord God Almighty
Jesus Christ.

The Third Joyful Mystery
THE NATIVITY

The glory of God has shone upon us:
his great power has appeared through the Virgin,
for the Almighty chose the humblest of births
to manifest through such humility
his all-powerful love.

In the city of David, a savior is born! The shepherds are invited to go find him.[1] The Magi in turn are called to set out to seek him.[2] Herod searches for him in the Scriptures—but only to have him killed.[3] Yet neither the shepherds nor the Magi would have been able to find and recognize the Word made flesh had God not guided them by the voices of angels or the sign of the star. Herod is forced to kill all the young children to be sure of reaching the King of eternal peace.[4] For him, the sentence of judgment is accomplished in advance: "Whatever you did for one of these least brothers of mine, you did for me."[5]

In the city of David, Mary reflects on this great mystery in her heart: in loving her newborn son, it is God himself she adores! Her child, her God: what a great mystery! It was Mary who first understood that "God so loved the world he gave his only Son."[6] And it was Mary who understood, before all others, that the first and second commandments are one and the same.

In heart to heart conversation with Mary, let us learn to seek, to find, and to love God in the people and circumstances he sets before us each day. May we learn that, in faith, "whoever does not love a brother whom he has seen cannot love God whom he has not seen."[7]

1- *Lk 2:8-12* 2- *Mt 2:1* 3- *Mt 2:3-4* 4- *Mt 2:16*
5- *Mt 25:40* 6- *Jn 3:16* 7- *1 Jn 4:20*

Prayer

*God our Father, you sent into the world your only Son
whom the Virgin Mary welcomed in her heart
before receiving him in her womb.
Grant that we may welcome Christ through faith
and make him manifest,
he in us and we in him, through lives
devoted to the work of love you entrusted to him.
He who lives and reigns with you in the unity of the Holy Spirit.*

The Nativity
*Pietro di Cristoforo Vannucci, called Perugino (c. 1448-1523), oil on wood, 103.5 x 57.9 in.
Panel from the Polyptych of Saint Augustine*

At a time when realism was triumphing and Michelangelo's school of classicism was seeking to recreate nature with a paintbrush, this work stands as a kind of "reactionary" manifesto for the artificiality of art. The faces here express no human emotions: no joy, exaltation, no rage, worry, or sadness, but rather a gentle, heavenly contemplation. For a soul who has never experienced prayerful meditation, no truth, no beauty will ever appear. These bodies do not convey the use of any preliminary nude sketches; rather they withdraw behind their chaste robes. The perspective is not natural, but perfectly calculated. The interaction among the different picture planes, from the horizon to the baby Jesus, creates a perfect equilibrium between an evocation of the Gospel story and its theological interpretation. Everyone finds his or her proper place within this spiritual landscape. Naked and at the very bottom of the composition, lying directly on the ground, the Son of the Most High makes himself the Most Low. Then, at an appropriate distance, Mary meditates upon what it means to be the Mother of God. Then Joseph, very slightly withdrawn behind her: he has accepted his adoption by the Son of God, that he, Joseph, should become his human father. Thus he extends his hands over the child, showing the deference with which he will act as his protector. Behind them rises a structure symbolizing the Church to be. She is inhabited by the Holy Spirit. Two angels adore the empty ground below them, soon to become the place where, until the end of the ages, the real but invisible presence of the child in the manger will live for ever. And it is there that, still today, each one of us can go and bow down to adore him. The geometric figures of its framework (a rectangle for humanity; an isosceles triangle for divinity) establish the new and eternal covenant between God and man. Lastly, we find the shepherds, representative of all men of good will. They wait at the threshold of the Church, which they will enter through holy baptism.

Referred to as the "Candlemas" flower because it blooms in early February, the snowdrop is most appropriate here. Its white bloom blossoming against immaculate snow has also earned it the name "flower of the purification" in honor of the purification of Mary at the time of the presentation in the Temple.

Known as an antidote for snake bites, in Christian culture the cornflower is the symbol of Christ's victory over evil. Here it evokes the New Eve who, through the grace of Christ, crushed the ancient serpent's head beneath her heel, as well as the proclamation of the aged Simeon: "My own eyes have seen the salvation which you have prepared in the sight of every people" (Lk 2:29).

HAIL TO THE LORD WHO COMES

Hail to the Lord who comes,
Comes to his temple gate!
Not with his angel host,
Not in his kingly state:
No shouts to proclaim him nigh,
No crowds his coming wait;

But borne upon the throne
Of Mary's gentle breast,
Watched by her duteous love,
In her fond arms at rest;
Thus to his Father's house
He comes, the heavenly Guest.

The Fourth Joyful Mystery
THE PRESENTATION IN THE TEMPLE

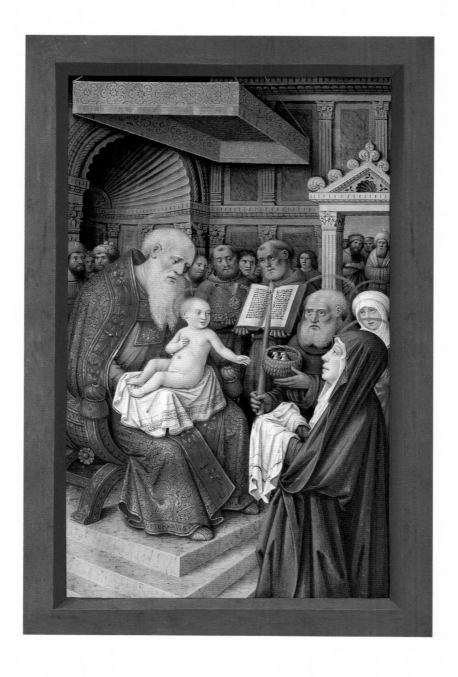

*The Virgin advanced
carrying in her arms the Son begotten before the dawn of time.
Simeon took him in his arms, announcing to the people
that this Child was the Savior of the world
and a light to the nations.*

On the appointed day, at the hour fixed by God, they meet: Mary, Joseph, Simeon, and Anna gather around the newborn.[1] The Temple is truly the place of the presence and the glory of God. And it is in this highly symbolic place that God beckons two elderly people to come forth to meet him. Simeon has been waiting, Anna has been watching. Both stand ready and receptive, in the stark simplicity of faith. Day and night in the Temple, they patiently keep vigil, hoping for a sign from God. And now the Spirit leads them across the Temple court into the glorious Presence veiled in the form of a little baby, asleep in the arms of his young mother. It is truly he, the *glory* and the *light to the nations*.[2]

In this joyful encounter, Mary and Joseph are filled with wonder, amazed by these strange words of blessing and praise. But the light of this day also foreshadows a drama that is already unfolding. For the prophet Simeon proclaims that Mary's heart will be pierced by a sword.[3] He thus makes clear how closely the Virgin Mary will be associated in her Son's work of salvation, to the point of giving her life for love. In this, Mary is the exemplary role model for Christians. Beyond all *contradiction*,[4] a Christian is one who keeps the flame of faith alive through his active love of others. The first contradiction, *that the thoughts of many may be revealed*,[5] is that offering your life for those you love surpasses all other sacrifices and spiritual paths.

In meditating upon this mystery, may we understand that the gift of self means following in the footsteps of Christ — falling down and then getting back up, again and again. And so we ask Mary to watch over us during the course of our earthly pilgrimage that, when we come to the hour of our death, we may receive the peace of the good and faithful servant, ready to enter into his Master's joy.

1- *Lk 2:27-28*   2- *Lk 2:29-32*   3- *Lk 2:35*
4- *Lk 2:35*   5- *1 Cor 12:31*

Prayer

God our Father,
in the Temple your humble servant Mary
presented the Author of the new Law to you.
Following her example,
grant that the Church may always keep this new covenant intact,
preserving an unblemished faith with ever stronger hope
and ever more ardent charity.
Through Christ our Lord.

The Presentation of Jesus in the Temple (1510)
Vittore Carpaccio (c. 1460-c. 1525), oil on wood, 165.3 x 90.9 in.

This altarpiece of the Presentation of Jesus in the Temple was executed in 1510 for a chapel of the Church of San Giobbe (Saint Job), the first Renaissance church built in Venice (1493). Carpaccio judged that the interior richness he had to transmit required the greatest modesty of expression. His artwork is thus charaterized by a sobriety of treatment and a freshness of palette which, seen in sunlight, confers an aspect of enamelwork, unlike the realism favored by Michelangelo at the time. Before an apse decorated with gilded mosaics reminiscent of the Cathedral of San Marco, the altar appears like a stage on which one of the actors—and not just any actor, but the littlest, the most humble, the most vulnerable—is God himself. In the foreground, on the frontier between the visible and invisible universes, like the celestial choirs at the Nativity, the angelic musicians attest that what is being played out on this earthly stage has a celestial dimension. Scenes summing up the history of salvation are embroidered on the chasuble of the elderly Simeon, robed as a priest.

Emblem of the universal love of the Virgin Mary, the rose here invites us to enter into a communion of emotion with the Mother of God as she reflects in her heart on all the things happening to her Son.

Through the violet color of the lilac we share in the anguish that must have gripped Mary and Joseph as they sought their Son for three days. But the branch of lilac is almost hidden by the greenery of the other flowers. Green, the color of hope, thus takes precedence over the tragic dimension of the color violet: Jesus will be found in the Temple.

The bellflower, associated by its shape with funeral bells, prefigures Christ's death, while the discreet primula, a springtime flower, already heralds the joy of the Resurrection. The presence of these two flowers opens our minds to an understanding of "the Father's affairs" (see Lk 2:49) to which Christ is to consecrate his life.

O MY JESUS

Soul: O my Jesus, I have lost you,
The night is dark and long,
And I have searched this whole night through
For you among the throng.

When I left old Jerusalem,
I thought you were beside.
Now I've searched every street and square,
This whole great city wide.

Jesus: Though times I seemed so far away
I never left your heart.
For in the temple of your soul,
We'll never be apart.

The Fifth Joyful Mystery

THE FINDING OF THE CHILD JESUS

*Blessed are those who hear the Word of God
and observe it.*

"Why were you looking for me? Did you not know that I must be in my Father's house?"[1] The Gospel notes that Mary and Joseph do not understand these words Jesus speaks to them. Later, when Jesus becomes an adult, his family goes looking for him.[2] At this Jesus exclaims, "Who is my mother? Who are my brothers? Whoever does the will of my heavenly Father is my brother and sister and mother."[3] And again, when a woman declares his mother blessed, Jesus responds, "Rather, blessed are those who hear the word of God and observe it."[4]

Often, a verse from the Gospel or an event in our life can unsettle us. We don't understand what God wishes to tell us or what he wishes to do. When things are beyond our comprehension, let us look to the Virgin Mary. She kept and reflected in her heart upon all those words so hard to hear, on all those events so difficult to bear.[5] A response of love alone can illumine all situations: "May it be done to me according to your word"[6]; "Not my will but yours be done."[7] Such a response on our part would be neither resignation nor fatalism, but rather a commitment to love to the end—heroically, if necessary, but above all discreetly, as Jesus does for thirty years while living with Joseph and Mary in a little village in the middle of nowhere.

Let us meditate with Mary: Our Lord was no less the Son of God and Savior of the world while carrying out the most insignificant tasks in the obscurity of his private life than when performing the most glorious works of his public ministry. Let us pray that, in our family, professional, and social lives, we may imitate the simplicity of life of the Holy Family.

1- *Lk 2:49* 2- *Mt 12:46-47* 3- *Mt 12:48-50*
4- *Lk 11:28* 5- *Lk 2:19* 6- *Lk 1:38* 7- *Lk 22:42*

Prayer

In your great wisdom, Father almighty,
you made the immaculate womb of Mary the Temple of your Word.
Grant that, following her example, we may meditate in the silence of
our hearts upon the mysteries of the life of your Son, Jesus Christ,
that, as we put into practice his new commandment,
we may hasten the coming of your kingdom.
He who lives and reigns with you in the unity of the Holy Spirit.

Christ among the Doctors (1st half of the 15th century)
Tempera and gold leaf on wood, 44 x 30 in.
Spanish School, Catalonia

This wood panel painted in the first half of the fifteenth century was undoubtedly the work of a disciple of the Catalonian master Bernardo Martorell. The anonymous painter chose to illustrate the moment when Mary and Joseph find Jesus in the Temple after three days of searching. In a medieval university lecture hall, the young Jesus stands at the professor's rostrum wearing the gown of a master of theology. His mother says to him, "Son, why have you done this to us? Your father and I have been searching for you with great anxiety." Jesus turns to his parents and replies, "Why were you looking for me? Did you not know that I must be in my Father's house?" (Lk 2:48-49). Mary and Joseph do not understand what their Son means. Yet their faces express attentiveness to what he says: in their confusion, they are still listening for him to enlighten them. But they will be given no further explanation. In a gesture reminiscent of the Noli me tangere, the child-God gives them to understand that there is a profound mystery here which many prophets had hoped to see but which even they could not have grasped, at least for the time being. They would first need to reflect on all these things in their hearts (see Lk 2:51). What an unfathomable mystery to be the parents of God! Facing them from their benches, the doctors of the Law are immersed in the Scriptures, rereading them from the perspective opened by the holy Child who is about to fulfill them. But it was to be a pagan, a centurion of the Roman army, who would cry out at the foot of the cross, "Truly this man was the Son of God!" (Mk 15:39).

Luminous
Mysteries

"This addition of these new mysteries,
without prejudice to any essential aspect of the prayer's
traditional format, is meant to give it fresh life
and to enkindle renewed interest in the rosary's place
within Christian spirituality as a true doorway to the depths
of the Heart of Christ, ocean of joy and of light, of suffering
and of glory. Each of these mysteries is a revelation
of the Kingdom now present in the very person of Jesus."

Blessed John Paul II
Rosarium Virginis Mariae 19 & 21

According to Greek mythology, the goddess Aphrodite, in grief over the death of her lover Adonis in a hunting accident, mingles her tears with the blood of the hero. From these drops of blood and tears the nymph Anemone is born. Having received life from a mortal wound, the anemone becomes the symbol of renewal and fertility. Convinced that even through a pagan culture the Holy Spirit has prepared hearts to receive the Gospel, the early Church sees in this myth a figure of baptism, for it is through the death of Christ that we are reborn to true life. It is thus that the anemone emerges as the sacred flower of baptism. What's more, the name "anemone" comes from the Greek *anemos*, meaning "the wind," and is thus associated with the Holy Spirit, who descends upon Christ at his baptism.

JESUS, WE FOLLOW THEE

Jesus, we follow thee,
In all thy footsteps tread,
And seek for full conformity
To our exalted Head.

Baptized into thy death,
We sink into thy grave,
Till thou the quickening Spirit breathe
And to the utmost save.

The First Luminous Mystery
THE BAPTISM OF THE LORD

The city of God rejoices in a river of living waters,
the holy dwelling of the Almighty.
Exultant with joy,
you shall draw water from the well of salvation!

At the baptism of Jesus, the entire Trinity reveals its glory.[1] In a flash of light on the banks of the Jordan, the Spirit attests that Jesus is the Son of the Father, the living Word sent into the world. And the voice of the Father resounds: "This is my beloved Son, with whom I am well pleased.[2] This is the One *in whom I have placed my love for you!*" And what love! A primordial, infinite, and unconditional love that goes to the depths of his entire being! A love which, to ransom us sinners, does not falter before the cost of his supreme baptism of blood and death, even death on a cross…

After baptizing the Lord, John will make his own the testimony of the Spirit who came down and remained upon Jesus: "Now I have seen and testified that he is the Son of God."[3] It is now our turn to witness to the Son of God in our time. The living waters of the Spirit flowing from the font of our baptism have transformed our inner life: may this "spring of water welling up to eternal life"[4] never cease to irrigate our faith, a faith acting in love, that we may "bear fruit that will remain."[5] Then, through the witness of our lives, may the world recognize us as truly beloved and loving sons and daughters of the same Father.

In contemplating the mystery of the baptism of Christ, let us ask Mary to teach us how to listen to the Word the Father speaks to us, so that each of us may shine with his limitless love. And may the world be filled with wonder: "See how they love one another!"[6]

1- *Mk 1:10-11* 2- *Mt 3:17* 3- *Jn 1:34*
4- *Jn 4:14* 5- *Jn 15:16*
6- Tertullian, *Apology 39, 7*

Prayer

Father most holy,
it was in the reality of our human flesh
that your only Son appeared to us.
As we recognize that, through Mary,
he was like us in his humanity,
allow our innermost hearts to be transformed by him
that we might bear in abundance
the fruits of the Holy Spirit.
Through Christ our Lord.

The Baptism of Christ (c. 1561)
Paolo Caliari, called Veronese (1528-1588), oil on canvas, 94.5 x 40.2 in.
Church of the Redeemer, Venice, Italy

Veronese settled in Venice around the year 1550. In 1561, Giovanni Battista Stravanzino and his father Bartolomeo commissioned from him this painting of the baptism of Christ for a little chapel, now destroyed. The commissioning patrons are pictured in the lower right-hand corner of the canvas. In the upper register of the painting, two putti open the earthly skies onto the divine universe. The voice of the Father is nothing but pure warm light, while the dove of the Holy Spirit is seen as Light proceeding from Light. Both John the Baptist and Christ adopt carefully posed positions; as though wishing to indicate his hesitation to baptize his Lord, and to witness to future generations that he acts on the command of his Master, the Precursor stands before him in humility and piety, almost submission—submission to his human destiny in the fulfillment of the Scriptures and with filial piety before the Father's plan of salvation. Only the two angels who emerge from the divine light can discern, in this image of a man bent down under the weight of the sins of the world, the Incarnation of eternal Love. They bow in adoration. One of them dips his foot in the waters of the Jordan—Yarden in Hebrew, "the lowest one" (because the Jordan is below sea level)—signifying that the lowest condition of man is not unworthy of the Almighty since God himself has immersed himself in it. This water of baptism, for ever sanctified by the one anointed here, is colorless, totally transparent—as transparent as it ever can be to the opacity of the human heart, of course, but already transparent to the divine light bathing the foot of the Savior.

Daisies are commonly associated with sentiments of love. White daisies
represent the purity of love, blue daisies extol the virtue of fidelity.
The cyclamen expresses enduring sentiments. Its buried tuber, which
allows it to survive the harshest of conditions, makes it the flower of
deep—meaning eternal—love. At Cana, marriage, restored to the grace
that the Father bestowed on it at the beginning of time, becomes an icon
of the union between Christ and the Church.
As we have already seen, the anemone is a symbol of fertility. Its violet
color here—a mixture of blue, the color of the sky, and red, the color of
the earth—further evokes the union between God and man.
Finally, the new and eternal quality of this union of love between God
and man is underscored in this bouquet by pansies with their five-petaled
flowers—for five is the number of the nuptial union between heaven
and earth.

All Praise to You, O Lord

All praise to you, O Lord,
Who by your mighty power
Did manifest your glory forth
In Cana's marriage hour.

You speak, and it is done;
Obedient to your word,
The water reddening into wine
Proclaims the present Lord.

Oh, may this grace be ours:
In you always to live
And drink of those refreshing streams
Which you alone can give.

The Second Luminous Mystery
THE WEDDING AT CANA

Blessed are you, Virgin Mary!
Through you, your Son worked the first of his signs;
through you, the Christ-Bridegroom prepared new wine
for his Bride, the Church;
through you, the disciples believed in their Master;
through you, the love between Christian spouses has been transformed.

In his benevolent plan, our Father wished that Mary be present at the mysteries of salvation. And so, at Cana, she is not only seated next to her Son, but humbly initiates divine revelation.[1] Seeing that the married couple have run out of wine to gladden the wedding festivities, Mary turns with faith to her Son. "Do whatever he tells you," she says to the servants.[2] And Jesus manifests his glory. In the midst of this feast, he makes new wine flow with the taste of eternity. He thus foreshadows the banquet in the kingdom when, at the appointed hour, he will rejoin his Bride, letting his heart be pierced so that the blood and water of eternal joy may run forth.[3]

By asking her Son to intervene, Mary opens up space for the transfiguration of the two great ecclesial vocations "for the sake of the kingdom of heaven"[4]: marriage and holy orders. The disciples, witnesses of this first manifestation of Jesus' mission, are transformed through faith and become Apostles. And, in the new covenant, having partaken of the wine of the eternal wedding banquet, "authentic married love is caught up into divine love."[5] Thus the love between spouses becomes capable of revealing "to the Church and the world the communion in love given by the grace of Christ."[6]

Through our meditation upon this mystery, may we remember that, whenever we are in need of something essential Mary is always by our side ready to help us. In her glory, she continues to assume the salutary role she played at Cana, that we may all one day know the joy of the new wine.

1- *Jn 2:3-6* 2- *Jn 2:5* 3- *Jn 19:34* 4- *Mt 19:12* 5- Paul VI, *Second Vatican Council, Gaudium et Spes 48* 6- Blessed John Paul II, *Familiaris Consortio 19*

Prayer

In your great wisdom, Father most holy,
you willed that the Virgin Mary, the Mother of our Lord,
be present at the mysteries of our salvation and,
first of all, at the great mystery of marriage.
Grant that we may faithfully follow
her guidance to do what your Son told us.
He who lives and reigns with you in the unity of the Holy Spirit.

The Wedding at Cana (13th century)
Stained-glass panel, positioned below Notre-Dame de la Belle Verrière
(1st bay of south choir ambulatory)
Cathedral of Notre-Dame, Chartres, France

Around 1233, the stained-glass windows were set in place in the newly constructed Chartres Cathedral, built in what was then known as the French style, having originated in central France (and since the seventeenth century referred to as "Gothic"). It was without doubt at this time that the Romanesque stained-glass window of the Virgin in Majesty, miraculously surviving a fire in 1191, was beautifully restored and enhanced with the inclusion of twenty new panels in a Gothic arched window. Given these extraordinary new proportions, it deservedly earned the name of Notre-Dame de la Belle Verrière ("Our Lady of Beautiful Glass"). The panel of the wedding at Cana, shown here, was one of these latter additions to this magnificent ensemble. The master glassmaker has illustrated the scene in which Mary tells the servants: "Do whatever he tells you" (Jn 2:5). Through her imposing stature, Mary is the focal point. Her wide-open eyes light up her remarkable face. She is truly the daughter of Zion awaiting with all her being the fulfillment of the Promise. The first covenant celebrated the union of God with his people; the new covenant renews that alliance in the wedding of Christ with the Church and thereby opens it to all mankind.

Great narrative stained-glass windows served as a kind of catechesis in the form of a picture book, conveying the message through coded symbolism. Here, the mother of Jesus holds a book of the Gospels, the Word of God par excellence. The message is clear: to do today what Jesus tells us to do, just as Our Lady of Chartres urges, is to do what is written in the Gospel.

The discreet presence of daffodils in this bouquet is a perfect evocation
of the preaching of the Lord: their golden hue affirms that the Word of
God is the only treasure worthy of our attachment, while their buried
bulb recalls that "the kingdom of heaven is like a treasure buried
in a field" (Mt 13:44).
The iris, the source of the heraldic fleur-de-lis, symbolizes Christ's
royalty and trumpets aloud the inauguration of the Kingdom of God.
Finally, the roses invite us to follow in the footsteps of Mary, she who
first believed in the coming of the kingdom, she who was ever the most
faithful of her Son's disciples.

Go, Tell It on the Mountain

He possessed no riches,
No home to lay his head;
He fasted in the desert,
He gave to others bread:

He reached out and touched them,
The blind, the deaf, the lame;
He spoke and listened gladly
To anyone who came:

He still comes to his people,
His life moves through the lands;
He uses us for speaking,
He touches with our hands.

The Third Luminous Mystery
THE PROCLAMATION OF THE KINGDOM

Blessed are the eyes that see what you see!
Many prophets and kings desired to see what you see,
but did not see it.

"Jesus went around all Galilee, teaching and proclaiming the Gospel of the kingdom and curing every disease."[1] Thus Saint Matthew sums up the public life of Jesus in three significant phrases.

Indefatigable, Jesus goes forth to meet men. Here he is; people look for him, but he has already moved on. He calls disciples, but only to send them, too, out on the road.

Jesus teaches, and his teaching is the proclamation of the Good News: "Blessed are the clean of heart,"[2] those who listen to his word, those who observe it, those who believe with humility, those who forgive, those who become disciples of the kingdom by doing the will of the Father and following Jesus with all their love.

The final proclamation has no need of words: it is there for all to see. With faith the size of a mustard seed,[3] the lame walk, the deaf hear, lepers are cleansed, the blind see, the dead are raised. Behold, the Kingdom of God is among us.[4]

The heart of Jesus' life and teaching is divine love communicated to man in word and deed. Announced along the roads of Galilee, this love will be revealed in all its fullness on the cross where it will be poured out till the end of time through the ministry of the Church.

With Mary, in contemplation of the mystery of the proclamation of the kingdom, let us ask for the grace to become true witnesses of divine love: simple and joyful, prompt to listen, generous in our response, and faithful to the end.

1- *Mt 4:23*   2- *Mt 5:8*
3- *Mt 17:20*   4- *Lk 17:21*

Prayer

Lord our God,
you gave us the Virgin Mary as the model of a disciple
who faithfully keeps the words of life.
Open our hearts that we may welcome your Word of salvation.
Through the power of the Holy Spirit,
may it bear fruit in abundance.
Through Christ our Lord.

Christ Calling Andrew and Simon Peter (detail of the south absidial vault, 14th century)
Fresco
Church of Saint John the Baptist, Origne, France

In the little village of Origne, in southwest France, the Church of Saint John the Baptist was built in the thirteenth century and partially remodelled in the seventeenth. Beneath the whitewashed interior of this modest edifice of simple design lay hidden a cycle of fourteenth-century frescoes featuring the lives of Saints Peter and Paul. This Christ Calling Andrew and Simon Peter is one of the paintings that were discovered in the 1970s and recently restored. At dawn, as the rosy bronze rays of the sun tinge the waters of Lake Tiberias, we find the Lord walking along its banks to meet two fishermen who have returned empty-handed from a night of fishing. Standing before them, he addresses Andrew and Simon Peter in their boat, "I call you to bear good news to all nations: I will make you fishers of men" (see Mt 4:19).
Yet the artist wished to show the Lord addressing at the same time all the faithful called by the Church to this holy place. He points with his finger to emphasize his words, like a teacher instructing by his own authority. Clearly holding up the book of the Gospels which contains all his teaching, Christ the divine Teacher is represented here, the One whom Clement of Alexandria describes as "the guide of childlike and simple souls who insists that we advance in wisdom and holiness rather than in science." It is in this truly childlike spirit that the artists in the time of the cathedrals worked, true Christian teachers if ever there were, whether architects, sculptors, painters, or stained-glass makers. And it is in this same childlike spirit that we must in our turn listen to the Master to become witnesses in the service of the New Evangelization.

What better flower than the heliotrope, sun born of the sun, to evoke the One who revealed himself in the broad daylight of the Transfiguration: God born of God, Light born of Light?

The aster, from the Greek meaning "shining star" because of the structure of its petals, is another flower of light. It symbolizes trusting love, like that which the disciples placed in Jesus.

The crocus recalls the saintly splendor in which Moses and Elijah are arrayed. It is from this flower that saffron is obtained (from the Arabic *asfar* meaning "golden yellow"). In medieval miniatures, saffron was used to gild the halos of the saints.

Finally, the geraniums here are known as "crane's bill" because of the elongated shape of their fruit. The crane confers the symbolism of the radiant peace of immortality.

QUICUMQUE CHRISTUM QUAERITIS

Quicumque Christum quaeritis,
Oculos in altum tollite:
Illic licebit visere
Signum perennis gloriae.

Illustre quiddam cernimus,
Quod nesciat finem pati,
Sublime, celsum, interminum,
Antiquius coelo et chao.

O ye who seek the Lord,
Lift up your eyes on high,
For there He doth the Sign accord
Of His bright majesty.

We see a dazzling sight
That shall outlive all time,
Older than the depth or starry height,
Limitless and sublime.

THE TRANSFIGURATION OF THE LORD

We hail you, Virgin Mary,
for you have given us
the Light of the world!

Having announced his Passion and death to the disciples,[1] Jesus took Peter, James, and John and led them up a mountain. There, in the presence of Moses and Elijah, "he was transfigured before them; his face shone like the sun."[2] What better way to show them who he was: God from God, Light from Light; what better way to indicate that his Passion and death would lead him to the glory of the Resurrection?

Here as in his baptism, God the Father witnesses to Jesus: "This is my beloved Son. Listen to him."[3] Thanks be to God, today as yesterday, that the Light from Light shines in the darkness. "Listen to him!"—Repent and believe in the Gospel[4] that the light of his life may shine in your hearts! "Listen to him!"—Jesus, God from God, has given you the power to become children of God. "Listen to him!"—You are children of light; live as children of the light!

Who is better suited than Mary to teach us how to listen to her Son? She helps us to remain at peace and untroubled, standing steadfast in the living light of the Gospel.

1- *Mt 16:24-28* 2- *Mt 17:1-2*
3- *Mt 17:5* 4- *Mk 1:15*

Prayer

Most holy Father,
we pray that the Church,
following the example of the Mother of Christ,
may gather up into her arms all her dispersed children,
so that enlivened by the one Spirit, they may become one Body,
transfigured by your glory, the Body of Christ.
He who lives and reigns with you in the unity of the Holy Spirit.

The Transfiguration (c. 1594-1595)
Ludovico Carracci (1555-1619), oil on wood, 172.4 x 105.5 in.

As the teachings of the Council of Trent were beginning to bear fruit, the Church became concerned about the course into which the Mannerists had strayed with their wild overuse of intellectual subtleties. She thus encouraged artists to produce religious works more immediately accessible to the faithful and more respectful of the letter of biblical texts according to the Vulgate. It was in response to this call that Ludovico Carracci, along with his cousins Agostino and Annibale, founded in 1585 the painting academy of the Incaminati ("those on the path"). As the inititators of the Baroque and Classicism, the Carraccis were the fathers of seventeenth-century European painting and, more widely, of all academic art to this day.
In this Transfiguration, Carracci puts to great effect a grandiose style which seeks first to impress the faithful viewer before it invites his contemplation. The beauty and variety of the lighting, the freshness and contrast of the colors, the voluminous folds of the drapery which further develop the figures, all contribute to the elaboration of this lyrical and sumptuous composition with its actors adopting almost forced poses. The point was to be as explicit as possible to the faithful. Moses, the founder, and Elijah, the restorer, are ostentatiously turned toward Jesus in order to show clearly that the path prepared by the old covenant leads ultimately to Christ. In the foreground, before this dazzlingly bright mystery, Saint John is plunged in prayerful contemplation, while Saint James expresses the fear of God. So stunned is Saint Peter that, without really knowing what he is saying, he speaks: "It is good that we are here... If you wish I will make three tents..." In reply, Jesus gestures to him to listen to the voice from on high. It will confirm Peter's admirable responses to the questions Jesus continually asks each of his disciples: "Who do you say that I am?" and "Do you also want to leave me?" And the heavenly Father witnesses: "Jesus is truly the Son of the living God, he alone has the words of eternal life."

What better evocation of the multiple riches of the sacrament of unity than this beautifully arranged bouquet. The poppy, which grows in the middle of cornfields, recalls the blood spilled by the Son of God for us in the sacrifice relived in each Eucharist. The spiral shape of the blue convolvulus is the symbol of eternal life: "Whoever eats my flesh and drinks my blood has eternal life" (Jn 6:54). Foxglove, also nicknamed "Our Lady's glove," expresses ardent love: through the Eucharist, Christ shows his love for us even to the supreme sacrifice. The gillyflower accentuates enduring faithfulness: Jesus is truly present in the Eucharist until the end of the age. What is probably a white buttercup is the flower Saint Louis brought back from the Holy Land along with relics of the instruments of the Passion. Its luminous white sheen recalls the glorified Body which we receive in communion. Pansies are considered the flowers of the Passion. Their three colors symbolize the three divine Persons. As so remarkably rendered in Rublev's icon of *The Hospitality of Abraham*, the entire Trinity is present at the Eucharist. Finally, in the language of flowers, the peony is placed in this bouquet as an attestation of truth.

TANTUM ERGO

Tantum ergo sacramentum
Veneremur cernui,
Et antiquum documentum
Novo cedat ritui:
Praestet fides supplementum
Sensuum defectui.

Genitori Genitoque
Laus et jubilatio
Salus, honor, virtus quoque
Sit et benedictio:
Procedenti ab utroque
Compar sit laudatio.
Amen.

Down in adoration falling,
Lo! the sacred Host we hail;
Lo! o'er ancient forms departing,
Newer rites of grace prevail;
Faith for all defects supplying,
Where the feeble senses fail.

To the everlasting Father,
And the Son who reigns on high,
With the Holy Spirit proceeding
Forth from each eternally,
Be salvation, honor, blessing,
Might and endless majesty.
Amen.

The Fifth Luminous Mystery
THE INSTITUTION OF THE EUCHARIST

Because there is one bread
we are one body,
for we all share in the same bread
and the same cup.

In the fourth Gospel, the disciple whom Jesus loved does not recount the institution of the Eucharist. But what he does tell us forms an inseparable complement to the story of the Last Supper which the other three Evangelists have passed down to us.

John's evocation of the washing of the feet in fact seeks to reveal the ultimate significance of the Eucharist:[1] Christ's mission does not end with the Ascension, but rather bears fruit in abundance across all time and space through the action of Christians. In a supreme beatitude, Jesus himself insists upon this dimension of the Eucharist: "Do you understand what I have done for you?... As I have done for you, you should also do. Blessed are those who do it."[2]

To carry on the work of Jesus, it was necessary for his disciples to receive communion in his body, to the point of becoming one Body — his Body. The consecrated bread and wine are until the end of time much more than mere symbols; they are truly the Body and Blood of Christ. In loving to the end those who are their own in this world, Christians accomplish a mission well beyond the imitation of Christ; their mission is truly the mission of Christ, kept alive and renewed throughout the ages. Within these two inseparable miracles lies the unique sacrament of the Eucharist, by which Christ gathers up humanity into his communion with the Father.

Before the infinite riches of the mystery of the Eucharist, Mary shows us how to conform our lives to the faith. She sets the example of the just equilibrium between grace received and the gift of self.

1- *Jn 13:1-17*   2- *Jn 13:13-17*

Prayer

Father most holy,
your only Son joined our human nature to his divine nature
in the womb of the Virgin Mary.
As we venerate her on this day, we beseech you:
may the sacrament of your love be for us the sign of unity
and the bond of charity.
Through Christ our Lord.

The Institution of the Eucharist *(detail, c. 1451-1453)*
Fra Angelico (c. 1387-1455)
Fresco
Cell 35, Convent of San Marco, Florence, Italy

On February 18, the date of his birth in heaven, Fra Angelico is memorialized in the Dominican martyrology as follows: "In Rome in 1455, Blessed Giovanni da Fiesole, known as the Angelic One, priest of the Order of Preachers, who, ever attached to Christ, expressed through his painting what he interiorly contemplated, to raise the souls of men to heavenly realities." This Florentine painter was beatified and named, along with Saint Luke, patron of artists by Pope John Paul II.

It was not a representation of Christ's Last Supper that Fra Angelico painted here on the walls of Saint Mark's convent, but rather a meditation on the renewal of the mystery of the Eucharist: communion in the Body of Christ as the source and summit of communal religious life, the nourishment and object of all prayerful life. We are not in the Upper Room, but in the monastery refectory. In this detail, the disciple Jesus loved crosses his hands over his chest in a sign of adoration; Saint Peter folds his hands in an act of thanksgiving.

Fra Angelico has thoroughly stripped down the decor of this Holy Communion administered by the Lord himself. There is nothing to encourage any distraction from the contemplation of the principal subject. The floor and back wall are bare, painted in earth tones that magnify the simplicity of the mendicant's life. There is no visible source of the light that envelops the scene; it creates no shadows other than those strictly necessary to the drawing. Bathed in this indwelling light, the colors and figures appear diaphanous. The idealized figures seem already to have taken on their glorified bodies. As Michelangelo once said of Fra Angelico: "This good monk has visited paradise and been allowed to choose his models there."

Sorrowful Mysteries

"From the beginning Christian piety… has focused on
the individual moments of the Passion,
realizing that here is found the culmination of the revelation
of God's love and the source of our salvation….
The sorrowful mysteries help the believer
to relive the death of Jesus, to stand at the foot of the cross
beside Mary, to enter with her into the depths of God's love
for man and to experience all its life-giving power."

Blessed John Paul II
Rosarium Virginis Mariae 22

"Father, if you are willing, take this cup away from me" (Lk 22:42).
What truth, attested by the peonies surrounding it, in this blood-red
tulip which stands out from the bouquet and bows down as it presents
itself to Christ! It is the chalice of Gethsemane into which will be poured
drops of the dying Jesus' sweat and blood; into which will flow the blood
and water from his pierced heart.
The cherry blossoms, symbol of self-offering, here attest with lovely
simplicity that "no one has greater love than this, to lay down one's life
for one's friends" (Jn 15:13).

THE VOICE OF MY BELOVED

Once I ached for thy dear sake:
Wilt thou cause me now to ache?
Once I bled for thee in pain:
Wilt thou rend my heart again?
Crown of thorns and shameful tree,
Bitter death I bore for thee,
And wilt thou have nought of me?

The First Sorrowful Mystery
THE AGONY IN THE GARDEN

Hail to you, Virgin Mary,
hope of all believers:
you come to the aid of the despairing,
you welcome all those who seek refuge in you.

In the dark depths of night, in the solitude of the garden, Christ Jesus calls out to his Father: "Abba, Father, all things are possible to you."[1] Like a little child, at the hour of death, he cries out in trust to his "Daddy." And the Father sends his angel to console his Son who is suffering the anguish of death.[2] The gentle caress of the Father, the humble trust of the Son... The cup of blessing today has a bitter taste, but, as yesterday, as always, Jesus surrenders himself into the hands of his loving Father.

But we poor sinners, to whom can we turn? Now and at the hour of our death, when we feel frightened, unworthy, hesitant—how can we beg our Father to take the cup of bitterness away? When our faith wavers at the moment we are confronted by the supreme baptism that we all must cross through to enter into Life—to whom can we turn when we know we are too weak to dare say in truth: "Father, not my will but yours"?[3]

At the hour of the anguish of our death, let us recall that Christ gave us his mother to be our mother.[4] We can take refuge in the arms of our heavenly Mommy. She is the hope of the humble and the lowly; she comes to the aid of the despairing; she comforts and consoles those suffering the throes of death, until the glorious day of her Son, our almighty God and Lord Jesus Christ, shines upon them. She is for ever the mother of the living.

1- *Mk 14:36*   2- *Lk 22:43*
3- *Lk 22:42*   4- *Jn 19:26*

Prayer

Most merciful Father,
you willed that the Virgin Mary shine on your Church
as a sign of sure hope:
grant comfort to those who are disappointed by life
and who seek refuge in her.
When they despair of their salvation, grant them renewed courage.
Through Christ our Lord.

Christ on the Mount of Olives (1819)
Francisco José de Goya y Lucientes (1746-1828)
Oil on wood, 18.5 x 13.75 in.
Colegio Escolapios de San Antón, Madrid, Spain

Unlike Goya's version from a decade or so earlier that is now in the collection of the Louvre, this little painting of Christ in the Garden of Gethsemane, dated 1819, is totally shrouded in black. Now is the hour of the abominable night, now is the hour of death which engulfs all. Death has chosen her victim, she approaches, she already has him in her sights. In the face of this monster bloodthirsty for life, the Man finds himself alone, infinitely alone, in terror of being crushed and for ever annihilated, obliterated. With arms opened wide in the shape of the cross, his face crying out to heaven the tragedy of the human condition, he implores the heavens for a glimmer of hope. It was in this hope that he had lived; it is in this same hope that now, hoping against hope, he wishes to die. For this reason he has donned a baptismal robe, the robe of the elect, made brilliantly white by a divine light which, nevertheless, does not scatter the advancing shadows. True man, the Son of Man cannot avoid this passage through the supreme baptism. Yet here is an angel proffering him not only a chalice in his left hand but, in his right hand, a ciborium as well. In this, Goya's interpretation corresponds to the Gospel texts which first refer to the chalice of the Passion presented to Christ, then to the consolation of an angel. Goya assimilates this angelic consolation to holy Viaticum, the final communion administered by the Church to those entering the throes of death and which he, sick unto death, now receives. But what is this food capable of consoling a man crushed by the fear of suffering and the terror of death? Jesus himself tells us: "My food is to do the will of the one who sent me" (Jn 4:34). Goya's painting, ushering us into the heart of Christ's own agony during which, through Viaticum, he receives the grace of communion with the will of his Father, elevates us to the heights of the Eucharistic mystery.

Goya. feit. año. 1819

From the little bells of the blue campanula one can almost hear a somber death knell tolling for the pilloried King of the Jews. The shape of this flower and the form of its pointed petals recall the spiked scourges that wounded the body of Jesus.

The herb bennet, whose name means "blessed flower," is also called the "blood herb"; it symbolizes spilled blood and was considered beneficial in the treatment of wounds. Lastly, the gardenia with its white petals and golden yellow heart evokes the infinite love of the Sacred Heart, that heart which, at the Passion, beat for us in the breast of the Man of Sorrows and which, after being pierced, would be glorified.

BY MY OWN SINS I SCOURGE YOU

By my own sins I scourge you,
O Savior of mankind.
By secret deeds of malice,
Your holy hands I bind.

O Jesus please forgive me,
For all that I have done.
I trust in your forgiveness,
And mercy ne'er outdone.

The Second Sorrowful Mystery
THE SCOURGING AT THE PILLAR

Hail to you, Mother of Sorrows,
Mother of Christ,
aid of the afflicted.

His executioners give Jesus a beating and he gives them a look of peace. Men tortured by interior violence torture his body, savaging it until blood flows forth to purify them. They wound the flesh of God who allows himself to be battered the better to console them. Unwittingly they knock upon the gate of heaven itself, so long closed to man. And Jesus the door allows himself to be pounded, until giving way under the relentless blows. He knows what they are unaware of: that their furious attack is hastening their moment of redemption, that the One they persecute has looked upon them, from the beginning of time, with a look of tenderness: "Father, they know not what they do."[1]

In order to enter more deeply into the mystery of the Passion, let us contemplate the mystical testament of Christ etched in letters of fire upon his body by the scourge: lash upon lash raining down upon him, wound after wound are so many stigmata that inscribe in his flesh his last will and testament. This testament, soon to be published in sight of all on Golgotha, will, at the thrust of a lance, be signed with a flourish of blood and water. Should we accept the offer to become its beneficiaries, we are promised salvation and are made coheirs of the kingdom of heaven. Why then should such a desirable testament still be considered a stumbling block to some, foolishness to others?[2] What if we were to gaze upon Christ's Passion with new eyes by contemplating and honoring it where it is lived today in the most dramatic and eloquent way: among all our fellow Christians throughout the world who are persecuted, mistreated, put to death through hatred of their witness to the faith?

We can contemplate the Passion in all its fullness only with the aid of our Lady. As her heart was pierced by the sword of compassion, she is able to teach us how to unite our sufferings to Christ, by standing in the light of his Resurrection which raises us up again and saves us.

1- *Lk 23:34*   2- *1 Cor 1:23*

Prayer

Lord God, overflowing with tenderness and mercy,
you reconciled the world to yourself through the Passion of your Son.
You placed his Mother by his side throughout his suffering,
thus establishing her as the refuge of sinners and the aid of Christians.
Grant us the protection of such a Mother
that we may experience the solicitude of your love,
especially when our fidelity to the Christian faith
brings trials and persecution.
Through Christ our Lord.

Christ Bound to the Column
Alonso Cano (1601-1667), oil on canvas, 63¾ x 39¾ in.

Following Goya, here in his turn Alonso Cano invites us to view the Passion as an unfolding of the Eucharistic mystery. He depicts the Lord bound to a column before being given up to scourging and abuse. His friends have fled; his executioners have gone to seek their tools of torture. He is once again alone, surrounded by darkness. Light issuing from somewhere above staves off the night. In chiaroscuro, his body stands exposed, as though on a stage. Or rather as an offering displayed on an altar. But his pose has nothing glorious about it: painfully bowed to his left, his head leaning on his shoulder, he contemplates within himself the fulfillment of the Scriptures.

Alonso Cano offers for our contemplation the body of the Son of Man before his disfigurement by torture. This is an all-too-human body, it is true, but as beautiful as that of Adam when first fashioned by the hands of God at the dawn of creation. It is not a question of entering into this image, but rather of observing the mystery of the faith: here is the mortal flesh of the Son of Man, the new Adam. It is to be crushed by suffering and destroyed by death. It will be lacerated by the sins of the world. And yet, the invisible is manifested in this visible body, the immeasurable within its confines, the holy within its disgrace, eternity within its approaching death. For it is truly this body of which the Lord has spoken: "This is my body, given up for you."

According to an ancient tradition, the crown of thorns was woven from the branches of the hawthorn, whose white flowers were splashed by a circle of red stains. Tradition also recounts that its red stamens had been tinged by the drops of blood that had pearled on the forehead of Jesus. The violet chironia recalls Christ's cloak at his Passion, its heart dashed with the luminous yellow of love divine.

O SACRED HEAD SURROUNDED

O sacred head, surrounded
By crown of piercing thorn!
O bleeding head, so wounded,
Reviled and put to scorn!
Death's pallid hue comes over you
The glow of life decays,
Yet angel hosts adore thee
And tremble as they gaze.

In this thy bitter passion,
Good Shepherd, think of me
With thy most sweet compassion,
Unworthy though I be:
Beneath thy cross abiding
For ever would I rest,
In thy dear love confiding,
And with thy presence blest.

The Third Sorrowful Mystery
THE CROWNING WITH THORNS

*The Virgin has given birth to the One
who is both man and God:
he has restored peace
to us by reconciling in himself
the extremes of both poverty and grandeur.*

"Behold, your king!"[1] declares Pilate. This proclamation, uttered by a pagan to the Jewish high priests, resonates like a divine revelation. The mock insignia bestowed by the jeering soldiers confirm this royalty: the purple cloak, the crown of thorns, the simple reed as scepter.[2] And Pilate goes further, nailing the indictment of his condemnation above the cross: "Jesus of Nazareth, King of the Jews."[3]

But what sort of king is this Jesus who allows his kingship to be the object of such derision? Before Pilate, Jesus insists that his kingdom is not of this world, and that his royal mission consists above all in testifying to the truth, the divine truth which enlightens all mankind.[4] This is the truth of the Kingdom of God which Jesus has come to inaugurate on earth; a kingdom founded on the beatitudes[5] and whose only law is the new commandment.[6] This King—imprisoned, afflicted, humiliated, wounded, dying—wants us to encounter him and honor him by loving, *with his love*, all those who are close to us along our earthly journey. But more than this, he wants us to draw close to the afflicted, the humiliated, the wounded, the imprisoned, and the dying, in order to love them. It is this truth that the King of the universe calls us to live, right now, today, that we may become citizens of the kingdom of heaven.

As we contemplate the crowning with thorns, let us ask Mary to open our hearts to welcome the poorest of the poor, for a creative charity to gather in the outcasts, to make haste to offer them the love of the humble and gentle King who, through us, comes to serve and comfort them.

1- *Jn 19:14*   2- *Jn 19:1-3*   3- *Jn 19:19*
4- *Jn 18:36-38*   5- *Mt 5:3-12*   6- *Jn 15:12*

Prayer

Almighty God, we humbly beseech you,
through the intercession of the Virgin Mary
whom you have given us as Queen,
may your all-powerful love triumph over our weakness
that the glory of your kingdom may be made manifest.
Through Christ our Lord.

The Crowning with Thorns *(detail of the Passion Altarpiece, c. 1510)*
Workshop of Champagne or Picardie
Polychromed limestone
Chapel of Notre-Dame de la Houssaye, Pontivy, France

Hidden within the walls of a chapel in the Breton hamlet of La Houssaye lies one of those treasures in which faith and art are so intimately wedded as to achieve the status of a masterpiece. Over its length of almost thirteen feet, sculpted in stone in very high relief, more than a hundred figures people these Stations of the Cross. This wonderful retable placed above the altar presents scenes that took place two thousand years ago and are renewed today on the altar at each Mass. Here, Christ has already been crowned with thorns, enthroned, and cloaked in gold. For his court, this mock king has nothing but torturers, their faces twisted with hate, who render him homage with blows to his back. These same men would no doubt have thrown themselves at his feet to bow slavishly before him had he deigned to reveal himself in glory in the company of twelve legions of angels. The Lord of majesty looks at us. His gaze speaks to us. It shows us the path to follow, that of the Son of God, when we ourselves are humiliated by violence or injustice. Crowned with thorns, he suffers abuse with a supernatural dignity befitting the Lord of the universe he truly is. In the garden, however, he knew fear, he knew anguish; under the weight of the cross he will collapse; tortured by the pain of the crucifixion, he will cry out in physical and moral pain. Yet never once throughout his Passion, in anguish or serenity, faced with exhaustion or torture, will Christ waver from responding not just without violence or hate—but with ever more love toward his tormentors. "Truly, this was the Son of God!" (Mt 27:54). Here, an angel hands him the "small scroll" which will be opened at the blast of the seventh trumpet of the Apocalypse. The angel of the last day attests: "The mysterious plan of God shall be fulfilled, as he promised to his servants the prophets" (Rv 10:7).

The dog rose is the symbol of Christ's patience throughout his Passion. This bouquet includes three to remind us of the three times Christ fell along the road to Calvary. The first dog rose, whose yellow color suggests energy, is still standing upright. With its bent stalk and curled up petals, the second seems bowed down under the weight of the cross. The third seems almost lost within the bouquet: its purple color, the symbol of involution—the passage from life to death—is a reflection of Christ's purple cloak during his Passion. Evening primrose, known for its properties of hardiness and resistance, seems to support these three dog roses. Its white flower, the color of innocence, recalls the intervention of Simon of Cyrene, who helped Jesus to carry his cross.

Finally, the delicacy of the lobelias contrasts with the otherwise oppressive character of this bouquet. They indicate the path to heaven, a path reflected in their color, beckoning to a horizon beyond the way of the cross.

STABAT MATER

Stabat Mater dolorosa
Juxta Crucem lacrimosa,
Dum pendebat Filius.

Quem maerebat, et dolebat,
Pia Mater, dum videbat
Nati paenas inclyti.

Quis est homo, qui non fleret,
Matrem Christi si videret
In tanto supplicio?

At the cross her station keeping,
Stood the mournful Mother weeping,
Close to Jesus to the last.

Christ above in torment hangs,
She beneath beholds the pangs
Of her dying glorious Son.

Is there one who would not weep,
Whelmed in miseries so deep
Christ's dear Mother to behold?

The Fourth Sorrowful Mystery
THE CARRYING OF THE CROSS

Hail to you, Virgin Mary,
pray for us poor sinners,
now and at the hour of our death.

On the road to Golgotha, the mystery of the hidden life of Jesus reaches the point of paroxysm. Never before has the King of glory allowed himself to be so crushed by the frailty of his mortal nature: "he was spurned and avoided by men, a man of suffering," "so marred was his look beyond that of man," "as one smitten by God."[1] This hour is an utter mystery—God seems to have forsaken himself! "For God made him to be sin who did not know sin."[2] All of his hopes seem eternally dashed, for despite his pleas for help, God appears to pay no heed.[3] O despair, O dark night of the soul, O bottomless pit into which is plunged the One who took on the infinite distress of guilty man! *My God, my God*—he no longer says "Father," no longer says "Abba"!—*why have you forsaken me?*[4] Great is the mystery of faith!

And it is precisely this man and no other—whose divine glory is shrouded in the annihilation of the body that is offered up for us—whom we are asked to recognize, adore, and serve in the Sacrament of the altar! Yet Jesus also asks us to discern this hidden divinity in the faces of the men and women we encounter today! In the great mystery of faith, with the Passion at its heart, there is neither distinction nor separation between the invitation to "do this in memory of me"[5] and the exhortation, "I have given you a model to follow, so that as I have done for you, you should also do"[6]: it is but a single summons—to lay down your life for those you love.[7]

Mary takes us by the hand along the road to Calvary. With her, let us meditate upon what it means to us today "to love to the end."

1- *Is 52:14; 53:3-4* 2- *2 Cor 5:21* 3- *Ps 22*
4- *Mt 27:46* 5- *Lk 22:19* 6- *Jn 13:15* 7- *Jn 15:13*

Prayer

Father of all goodness,
you sent your only Son into the world
to become the Man of Sorrows,
hear the prayer we raise to you
through the intercession of the Virgin Mary.
Show us that our suffering is not in vain
when it is endured in union with the Passion of Christ,
for our salvation and that of our brothers and sisters.
Through Christ our Lord.

Christ and the Cyrenian (detail, 1547)
Tiziano Vecellio, known as Titian (c. 1488-1576), oil on canvas, 67.4 x 30.33 in.

Born at the end of the fifteenth century, Titian died, paintbrush in hand, toward the end of the sixteenth century, at the age of eighty-eight. This Christ and the Cyrenian is thus a work by the artist at the height of his powers. Of small dimensions, it was destined for private devotion during a period in which the faith was beginning to be a more individual, less communal, practice and a work of art was sought solely for its formal beauty. His own spiritual individualism allowed Titian to express his subjectivity in his work. Through vibrant brushwork that dissolves the contours of his forms, he manages to render almost physically palpable the drama played out here. Titian creates a portrait of incomparable veracity, grounded in extremely subtle psychological analysis. Out of his bloody countenance, through his tears, Jesus speaks straight to the heart of the viewer. Of his powerful arm and outstretched hand he makes an unassailable bulwark against the cross, so that it may not crush us. His expression, however, conveys only profound serenity: no reproach, no compassion, not even pain. He turns his face to ours, as if saying, "You who look at me, do not forget: it is to ensure your happiness that I suffer; I die that you might have life." His gaze says it all; it says: "You whose eyes meet mine, do you love me?"

The pansy is the flower of the Passion of Christ: the number of its petals recalls the five wounds, while its three colors make it an icon of the Trinity. With its spiked petals, the carnation evokes the nails of the crucifixion. But, more generally in Western art, the carnation, whose name in Greek means "flower of God," is a floral attribute of Christ, symbolizing the victory of love over death.

Because of its winding stem, the cyclamen bears a name that in Greek signifies "circle." Because it is without beginning or end and forms a whole, the circle is the symbol of divine eternity. At the moment of Christ's death on the cross, when the earth is covered in darkness, the luminous white brightness of this flower prefigures the light of the Resurrection.

WHEN I SURVEY THE WONDROUS CROSS

When I survey the wondrous cross
On which the Prince of glory died,
My richest gain I count but loss,
And pour contempt on all my pride.

Forbid it, Lord, that I should boast
Save in the death of Christ, my Lord;
The vain things that now tempt me most,
I sacrifice them to his blood.

The Fifth Sorrowful Mystery
THE CRUCIFIXION

Close by the cross of Christ
stands his mother Mary.
O Jesus, through your cross
you have redeemed mankind.

Terrified, shaken, the disciples flee in fear. Only *the disciple whom Jesus loved*[1] remains with the women and Mary, standing in sorrow. Divested of all, Jesus makes one last act of renunciation: he takes leave of his role as son and hands his mother a new child, the beloved disciple.[2] In this instant, through the mouth of his Son, God asks Mary once again to become a mother, the mother of the new humanity which is now being born and which will for ever witness to the love of God.

It is finished![3] Christ Jesus has brought to fulfillment the labor of love which the Father had entrusted to him. Death can now do its work, unaware that in devouring the Living One, it destroys itself. The man whom death had thought to have ensnared has escaped! He has placed his life and the life of all mankind back into the hands of the Father. His death on the cross now becomes the eternal sign of reconciliation and the gateway to everlasting life.

And behold—the stroke of a lance by which death had thought to put a final end to all hope.[4] Yet it is living Love which flows forth from the pierced heart of Jesus. Water, source of baptism, and blood, source of the Eucharist—blood and water that will give birth to the Church: a new people born of God's unconditional love for man.

At the foot of the cross, let us remain with Mary and contemplate the mystery of our filial adoption. Our new life as sons and daughters of God has no other source than the self-offering of Christ on the cross, giving us access to the resurrection, for the glory of God and the salvation of the world.

1- *Jn 13:23* 2- *Jn 19:25-27*
3- *Jn 19:30* 4- *Jn 19:33-37*

Prayer

Lord, Father most holy,
through the paschal mystery you established the salvation of humankind.
Grant that we may be counted among your adopted children
whom Jesus entrusted to his Virgin Mother as he died on the cross.
He who lives and reigns with you in the unity of the Holy Spirit.

The Crucifixion (1392-1393)
Piero di Giovanni, called Lorenzo Monaco (c. 1370-c. 1424)
Tempera and gilding on wood, 19.7 x 10.6 in.

Lorenzo Monaco—"Lawrence the Monk"—entered the Camaldolese (reformed Benedictine) convent of Santa Maria degli Angeli in Florence at the age of twenty. He was soon placed in charge of the workshop of the illumination and painting of manuscripts. Fra Angelico was among his students. This powerfully original crucifixion combines very different styles and techniques. Calvary, surprising in its most pure Byzantine style, symbolizes the new Sinai where the old and the new covenants meet. In the background, the earth opens to be made fertile by the golden sun of divine realities. The lance and the branch of hyssop bearing the sponge soaked in vinegar symbolize the stages of the Passion. Two angels gather the blood of Christ in golden chalices. At the top of the cross is the fresh green regrowth of the tree of life. Enthroned in its foliage is the pelican with its stricken breast, symbol of the Eucharistic Christ who gives to his own in this world his own body and blood as food and drink. In its enchanting purity, this work is one of the most beautiful meditations on the Eucharistic mystery that art has ever produced. And there is no better aid for the contemplation of this work in all its mystical richness than the Adoro te devote, a hymn composed by Saint Thomas Aquinas for the Feast of Corpus Christi:

Godhead here in hiding, whom I do adore,
Masked by these bare shadows...
On the cross thy Godhead
made no sign to men,
Here thy very manhood
steals from human ken:
O thou our reminder of Christ crucified,
Living Bread, the life of us for whom he died.

Bring the tender tale true
of the Pelican;
Bathe me, Jesu Lord, in
what thy bosom ran–
Blood whereof a single drop
has power to win
All the world forgiveness
of its world of sin.

Glorious Mysteries

"The... glorious mysteries ought to lead the faithful
to an ever greater appreciation of their new life in Christ....
The glorious mysteries thus lead the faithful to greater hope
for the eschatological goal towards which they journey
as members of the pilgrim People of God in history.
This can only impel them to bear courageous witness
to that 'good news' which gives meaning
to their entire existence."

Blessed John Paul II
Rosarium Virginis Mariae 23

This cheerful and luminous bouquet combines white laurel with convolvulus. Laurel, emblem of victory and glory, now crowns Christ, victorious over death. Its white flowers reflect the light of Easter; its evergreen foliage, immortality.

Convolvulus, also called morning glory, is none other than the "lily of the fields" of which Jesus spoke in the Gospels: "Learn from the way wild flowers grow.... Not even Solomon in all his splendor was clothed like one of them" (Mt 6:28-29). The lily of the fields here symbolizes the triumph of humility: on Easter morning, sweet Jesus, gentle of heart, is glorified for ever.

REGINA CAELI

Regina Caeli, laetare, alleluia:
quia quem meruisti portare, alleluia.
Resurrexit, sicut dixit, alleluia.
Ora pro nobis Deum, alleluia.

℣. Gaude et laetare, Virgo Maria, alleluia.
℞. Quia surrexit Dominus vere, alleluia.

Queen of Heaven, rejoice, alleluia.
For he whom you did merit to bear, alleluia.
Has risen, as he said, alleluia.
Pray for us to God, alleluia.

℣. Rejoice and be glad, O Virgin Mary, alleluia.
℞. For the Lord has truly risen, alleluia.

The First Glorious Mystery
THE RESURRECTION

Rejoice, Virgin Mary, mother of light!
Your Son Jesus, the Sun of Justice,
victorious over the shadows of the tomb,
illumines the whole universe, alleluia!

Alleluia! Christ is risen! The Son of the Virgin Mary, the Savior of the world, is truly risen! Easter day is a day of unique joy, light, and life: the Lord has dissipated the night of death and will never cease to fill the whole universe with rejoicing. Alleluia!

On Easter morning, the disciples' hearts leap with inexpressible joy to find their Lord—alive again.[1] And as we contemplate the mystery of the Resurrection of the Lord, poor sinners that we are, we marvel to discover that the Passover of the Lord touches us. It changes everything in our lives. This day is a day of celebration and rejoicing! By his rising, Christ has opened to us the treasures of salvation and grace.

The Father's plan has been fulfilled. The Son sent by God came to save all men from sin and has bestowed upon them, through grace, the gift of becoming children of God. And so we are! The death of Jesus on the cross has washed us and set us free from all sin. His Resurrection has won for us adoption as his brothers and sisters. It is true and such is our faith: from now on, through the grace of the Resurrection, we participate in the life of the Only Begotten Son. We are all children of the same Father, sharing our love for one another in communion with the Holy Spirit! Alleluia!

To increase our joy in contemplation of this mystery, let us stay close to Mary and listen to her sing with ineffable joy at finding her immortal Son again. Mary, mother full of grace, in receiving her Son receives the multitudes of his brothers and sisters.

1- *Mt 28:8*

Prayer

Father of eternal joy,
you gave life to the world
through the Resurrection of your Son Jesus.
Grant that we may one day share in the joy of eternal life
where Mary, our Blessed Mother,
stands waiting for us in the midst of her children.
Through Christ our Lord.

The Resurrection *(detail, c. 1570)*
Paolo Caliari, called Veronese (1528-1588)
Oil on canvas, 53.5 x 41 in.

To represent the Resurrection, early Christian artists were content to encircle the Holy Chrismon (Chi-Rhô) in a woven crown to symbolize the triumph of Christ over death. The fifth century in the East, and the sixth in the West, saw the first representations of the exact moment of the Resurrection of Christ, who is often shown being drawn out of the tomb by the hand of God himself. In the twelfth century, Christ could be seen standing in an open sarcophagus, and later, suspended above it. Veronese imagined the Resurrection as a kind of dazzling explosion haloing the body of Christ in a mandorla of light and propelling him, victorious, into the heavens. The tomb guards are literally overwhelmed by the blast and radiance of the phenomenon. In this supreme moment when, like a living flame of love, the paschal victim is raised in the perfect offering, the Son of God turns his gaze toward his Father, henceforth our Father, in a sublime expression of an act of thanksgiving (eucharistia in Greek). In the background, proud architectural ruins symbolize the end of the first covenant in the destruction of the Temple of Jerusalem, but even more they symbolize the ruins of the ancient Tower of Babel, whose mad dream is yet realized, beyond all vain human illusions: reunited in one Body by the sacrament of unity, humanity already receives a foretaste of its elevation to the highest heavens. Infinite love of our Father, supreme evidence of his tenderness, which makes us communicants in the victory of his Son.

The Greeks considered the mallow the flower of the elevation of the soul. As its color, mauve, was difficult to obtain, it was reserved in ancient Rome for the ornamentation of the triumphs of emperors and its most glorious generals.

The trumpet vine is a climbing plant that grows toward the sun. The two colors of this flower invite our meditation of the two natures of Christ, true God and true man. The silhouette of the flower is curiously similar to the shape of a trumpet, a fact which earned it its name. It thus recalls the acclamations that accompanied the Ascension of the Lord: "God goes up with shouts of joy; the Lord goes up with trumpet blast" (Ps 46:6)— and, of course, the trumpets of the Apocalypse which will resound when he comes again in glory.

ALLELUIA, SING TO JESUS

Alleluia! Sing to Jesus,
His the scepter, his the throne;
Alleluia! His the triumph,
His the victory alone:
Hark! The songs of peaceful Zion
Thunder like a mighty flood;
Jesus, out of every nation,
Has redeemed us by his blood.

Alleluia! Not as orphans
Are we left in sorrow now;
Alleluia! He is near us,
Faith believes, nor questions how;
Though the cloud from sight received him
When the forty days were o'er,
Shall our hearts forget his promise,
"I am with you evermore"?

The Second Glorious Mystery
THE ASCENSION

You are worthy of all praise, Blessed Virgin Mary,
you gave birth to Christ, our God,
who is now taken up in glory.

The skies open and Jesus disappears from the sight of the Apostles.[1] He has returned to the bosom of his Father. In contemplating this mystery, let us try to glimpse the love which, from before the foundation of the world and for all eternity, unites the Father and the Son in communion with the Holy Spirit… In his movement of Ascension to the Father, Christ Jesus raises the reconciliation between God and man to participation in this divine love!

But let us now follow the counsel of the angels and not stand gazing into the sky.[2] For now is the hour for the fulfillment of Christ's command: "Go, therefore, and make disciples of all nations."[3] It matters little that such a task is extraordinary, enormous, infinite! "Whoever believes in me will do the works that I do, and will do greater ones than these, because I am going to the Father."[4]

Christ raised in glory does not abandon his brothers, for he promises, "I am with you always, until the end of the age."[5] He sends them out to continue his work while remaining mysteriously present in them and through them. The Ascension of the Lord renders effective the bond that unites Christ and his disciples. He *remains* in them as long as they *remain in him.*[6] This communion of being and action makes it possible for us, disciples that we are, to accomplish today the works of the Father. Christians are none other than *alter Christi*, other Christs. Is this truth borne out in our own lives?

Meditating upon the mystery of the Ascension leads us into the movement of love spreading out to infinity. Mary is the privileged witness of this outpouring of divine grace, she whose humble "yes" has opened the gates of heaven for us.

1- *Acts 1:9*   2- *Acts 1:11*   3- *Mt 28:19*
4- *Jn 14:12*   5- *Mt 28:20*   6- *Jn 15:4*

Prayer

Eternal and Almighty God,
as we await the return in glory of your Son,
you have given us his Mother,
the Virgin Mary, as the protection of all who call upon her name.
Grant through her intercession that we may remain strong in faith,
firm in hope, and unstinting in charity.
Through Christ our Lord.

The Ascension (c. 1460-1464)
Andrea Mantegna (1431-1506), tempera on wood, 34 x 16.75 in.

Andrea Mantegna was the great initiator of the Renaissance in northern Italy. Called to Mantua by Ludovico Gonzaga, he became the official court painter there in 1460 before the age of thirty. This Ascension of Christ dates from that period.
In a rocky desert landscape, a version of the holy mountain depicted in icons, Christ is carried up to the sky by a cloud of cherubim. In his left hand he holds the banner of the triumphal cross: "On that day the root of Jesse shall stand as an ensign to the peoples; him shall the nations seek, and his dwellings shall be glorious" (Is 11:10, RSV). Gazing down on his disciples as he rises from their sight, his look seems to say, "I commit my work into your hands until I come again." His right hand raised like a scepter seems to underscore this parting commission and to bless them at the same time. On the ground, the disciples surrounding Mary stretch with all their being toward the heavens, not wishing to miss a moment of this last visible presence of the Lord. There are twelve of them: Matthias, in the lower right, has filled the place left by Judas, because he had followed Jesus "from the baptism of John until the day on which he was taken up from us" (Acts 1:22). Mantegna treats this scene as though he were painting ancient statues. The figures are powerful, static, almost arid sculptures. There is no attempt to charm; the artist deliberately refuses to play upon the emotions of the viewer. Because the artist keeps this distance, the mystery of faith retains all its power of truth. These hieratic figures are quite rightly depicted as immortalized. Christ in his human form is about to be received back into the bosom of God. And all men acquire along with him an inconceivable, indeed, an infinite dignity. The Ascension attests that, after Jesus, human nature no longer knows any limits: it is henceforth enthroned at the right hand of the Father.

In Greek, the word *phlox* means "flame." The color of its flowers gives
this bouquet the effervescence of a fire, a fire whose different sparkling
elements call to mind the tongues of flame which, in the Upper Room,
descended upon Mary and the Apostles.
This bouquet causes us to raise our voices in a hymn of prayer that the
Holy Spirit may descend upon us:
Fire of God, undying flame,
Spirit who in splendor came,
Let your heat my soul refine,
Till it glows with love divine.

HOLY SPIRIT, LORD OF LIGHT

Holy Spirit, Lord of light,
From the clear celestial height
Thy pure beaming radiance give.

Come, thou Father of the poor,
Come with treasures which endure;
Come, thou light of all that live!

Thou, of all consolers best,
Thou, the soul's delightful guest,
Dost refreshing peace bestow;

Thou in toil art comfort sweet;
Pleasant coolness in the heat;
Solace in the midst of woe.

Light immortal, light divine,
Visit thou these hearts of thine,
And our inmost being fill:

If thou take thy grace away,
Nothing pure in man will stay;
All his good is turned to ill.

Heal our wounds, our strength renew;
On our dryness pour thy dew;
Wash the stains of guilt away:

Bend the stubborn heart and will;
Melt the frozen, warm the chill;
Guide the steps that go astray.

Thou, on us who evermore
Thee confess and thee adore,
With thy sevenfold gifts descend:

Give us comfort when we die;
Give us life with them on high;
Give us joys that never end.

Amen. Alleluia.

The Third Glorious Mystery
THE DESCENT OF THE HOLY SPIRIT

You are the glory of Jerusalem,
the joy of Israel,
you are the queen of the Apostles,
the model of the Church,
holy Mother of the Lord.

Secretly inhabited by the beneficent presence of the Holy Spirit who overshadowed her at the Annunciation, Mary is present praying in the midst of the Apostles. With them she is bathed in the living flame, enveloped in the whirlwind of the divine breath.[1]

United with Mary, the nascent Church receives the gift of the Holy Spirit, the power of love inseparable from the Father and the Son — the Spirit of unity who gathers the members of the Church together in one Body; the Spirit of holiness who communicates the holiness of God himself; the Spirit of truth who teaches all things; the Spirit of power who sends them out to follow in the footsteps of Christ. Clothed with power from on high, the infant Church, with one heart and one soul, goes forth to announce the Gospel of life to the entire world.

Nothing has changed! Baptism, confirmation, and the sacramental life enable us to receive and unceasingly renew our openness to the gift of the Spirit. The one and only Spirit in myriad manifestations: the Spirit of wisdom and of understanding, the Spirit of counsel and of strength, the Spirit of knowledge and of fear of the Lord, the Spirit of love and charity...[2] One and the same Spirit who, today as yesterday, spurs the Church on to bear witness. To those who seek to silence them from proclaiming the Gospel, the Apostles reply, "It is impossible for us not to speak!"[3] So also for us; we cannot keep silent about the grace that fires our life.

Let us ask Mary to pray with us as she prayed on the day of Pentecost, that the Spirit may awaken in us the source of faith and propel us into the world to proclaim the joy of salvation and new life.

1- *Acts 2:1-4*   2- *Is 11:2*   3- *Acts 4:20*

Prayer

God, who sent the Holy Spirit upon the Apostles
when they were praying with Mary, the mother of Jesus,
grant us, through your intercession,
to work through word and example
for the triumph of your mission of love.
Through Christ our Lord.

Pentecost (c. 1611-1613)
Juan Bautista Maíno (1581-1649)
Oil on canvas, 112.2 x 64.2 in.
Panel from an altarpiece of the Monastery of Saint Peter Martyr in Toledo, Spain

Juan Bautista Maíno is one of the most important, and unjustly overlooked, figures of seventeenth-century Spanish painting. He was a student of El Greco, the friend and confidant of Velázquez, and a counselor to kings, but out of Christian humility he refused to put himself forward or, when he gained prominence in spite of himself, to profit from the fruits of his fame. In 1613, at the age of thirty-two, he settled in Toledo and became a friar preacher in the Dominican convent of Saint Peter Martyr. There he embarked upon the execution of an altarpiece of impressive proportions for the decoration of the chapel choir. This work devoted to Pentecost was one of its panels. We find ourselves here at the heart of the Upper Room fifty days after the Resurrection. Eleven Apostles, Mary the mother of Jesus, and Mary Magdalene are present. Only our Lady, with hands joined, remains in an attitude of fervent prayer. The Holy Spirit had already come down upon her to overshadow her; she gave birth to the Savior who sent the Holy Spirit. Henceforth and to the end of time, the Mother of God will bear the prayers of men to her Son, while the Apostles will begin their mission in the world. In a calculated anachronism, Luke is also present, though seated next to the gathering rather than a part of it. He is dressed in seventeenth-century Spanish clothing and wears glasses. He has clearly just finished writing the third Gospel and is beginning the Acts of the Apostles, the Gospel of the Holy Spirit, as dictated by John who is undoubtedly recounting the episode of the Ascension to him. Brother Juan Bautista here offers us his self-portrait in the guise of Saint Luke, patron saint of painters. On the floor in the foreground, the key to the kingdom of heaven lies waiting to be grasped by Saint Peter: the age of the Church is about to begin. With a clap of thunder, the Holy Spirit is made manifest here in flames of love which come to rest upon each one, setting them all ablaze.

For Saint Ambrose, the rose is the exclusive emblem of the Virgin Mary. Saint Bernard referes to Mary as the "rose without thorns"; in the Litanies of Loreto, the Virgin is given the symbolic title "Mystical Rose"; and it is no coincidence that, in honor of the Virgin Mary, Christians recite the "rosary"— two hundred Hail Marys offered like so many roses to the Queen of angels.

In this bouquet, the white rose celebrates the virginity of Mary, while the pink ones point to her femininity raised up to God through the grace of the Assumption. As for the golden yellow roses, they evoke the glorious mysteries to be culminated in the coronation of the Mother of God.

MEMENTO, RERUM CONDITOR

Memento, rerum Conditor,
Nostri quod olim corporis
Sacrata ab alvo Virginis
Nascendo formam sumpseris.

Maria Mater gratiae,
Dulcis Parens clementiae,
Tu nos ab hoste protege,
Et mortis hora suscipe.

Iesu, tibi sit gloria,
Qui natus es de Virgine,
Cum Patre, et almo Spiritu
In sempiterna saecula.

Remember, O Creator Lord!
That in the Virgin's sacred womb
Thou wast conceived, and of her flesh
Didst our mortality assume.

Mother of grace, O Mary blest!
To thee sweet font of love, we fly;
Shield us through life, and take us hence
To thy dear bosom when we die.

O Jesu! Born of Virgin bright!
Immortal glory be to Thee;
Praise to the Father infinite,
And Holy Ghost eternally.

The Fourth Glorious Mystery
THE ASSUMPTION OF MARY

Rejoice, glorious Virgin,
most beautiful among women!
Hail to you, woman dressed with the sun,
Queen crowned with twelve stars!

O Mary, new Eve without sin, your humility vanquishes the pride of the first woman; your faith conquers her doubt; your simplicity of heart foils the ruses of the ancient serpent. Through your "yes,"[1] you conceive by the Holy Spirit the One who would reopen the gates of heaven once closed by original sin. United with Joseph, your chaste spouse, you give birth to and raise the Savior of the world, our Lord Jesus Christ. Mother of God, who cooperate in an incomparable way in the work of your only Son, you are our Mother in the order of grace.

Woman guided by God, you unceasingly intercede for us poor sinners, just as you interceded at the wedding at Cana.[2] Woman adorned by God in a mantle of sun, your shining example is a light to guide our feet along the narrow path that leads to the kingdom of heaven.[3] Woman given by God to the pilgrim Church on earth, your maternal love makes you attentive to the prayers of all your children. Woman crowned with twelve stars, you are the star that leads us through the perils and anguish of this valley of tears until we at last reach our celestial home.

In contemplating the glory of your Assumption, Virgin Mary, we entrust ourselves to your maternal love. Mother of mercy, be our advocate before our only Mediator and Savior, your Son Jesus Christ, our brother and our God.

1- *Lk 1:38*   2- *Jn 2:3*   3- *Rev 12:1*

Prayer

Eternal and almighty God,
you assumed Mary,
the Immaculate Mother of your Son, into the glory of heaven.
Through her intercession,
grant that, after a life given in love,
we may be found worthy to receive our inheritance
in the kingdom that you have prepared for us
since the foundation of the world.
Through Christ our Lord.

The Death and Assumption of the Virgin (c. 1432)
Fra Angelico (c. 1387-1455), tempera and gold on wood, 24.33 x 15.2 in.

We are here in the fifteenth century, when formal definition of the dogmas of the Immaculate Conception (1854) and the Assumption (1950) had yet to consolidate the iconography of the passage of the Virgin Mary to heavenly life. This small panel was inspired by the De Transitus Sanctae Mariae, a sixth-century compilation of all the earliest sources of the tradition. Summoned by the Holy Spirit, the Apostles hasten from far and wide to Mary's bedside in Jerusalem. When they are all gathered around her, Mary relinquishes her soul to Jesus who, having come expressly for this purpose, bears her soul to heaven. The Apostles then carry her bier to a new tomb. On the third day, her body is taken up to heaven.

In the lower register of the panel, Fra Angelico represents a scene similar to that of final absolution as it was practiced at funerals of the time. The twelve Apostles, plus Saint Paul and Saint Luke, the biographer of the Virgin, surround the lifeless body of Mary. In the center, Christ has received the holy and immaculate soul, depicted in his arms as an adorable little girl. Saint Peter, in liturgical papal vestment with pallium, chants the Libera me, while next to him another Apostle holding an aspersorium proceeds to the rite of blessing with holy water. Four other Apostles are already preparing to raise the unblemished and precious body. Final absolution of the sins of the departed is not a contradiction of faith in the Immaculate Conception of the Virgin Mary; on the contrary, it is a consecration of her blessed humility. For in much the same way, the most pure Virgin had voluntarily submitted to the rite of purification at the Temple.

In the upper register, Fra Angelico represents the celebration in heaven when Mary, in body and soul, is welcomed into paradise by her divine Son as the celestial host of angels sing hymns to her luminous beauty. In an affirmation that the glorification of this humble maidservant of the Lord is truly a triumph of humility, Fra Angelico paints her with open arms—the same gesture with which she welcomed the will of God at the Annunciation.

If nothing better evokes the Assumption of the Virgin Mary than a
bouquet of roses, what could be more fitting than this queen of flowers
to celebrate the coronation of the Queen of Heaven. It is in a similar
sense that the rosary symbolically comprises four chaplets woven of roses,
with which the Virgin Mary is successively crowned.

The clematis is considered the symbol of spiritual beauty. In the language
of flowers, it bears a message of joy and light-heartedness. According to
one apocryphal tradition, during the flight into Egypt, the Holy Family
rests in the shade of this climbing plant. The collarette of the crowned
anemone is reminiscent of the royal diadem the Virgin Mary receives
from her Son in the glory of heaven.

O Gloriosa Domina

Hail most high, most humble one!
Above the world; below thy Son,
Whose blush the moon beauteously mars
And stains the timorous light of stars.

He that had made all things, had not done,
Till He had made Himself thy son.
The whole world's Host would be thy guest
And board Himself at thy rich breast.

Glory to Thee, great virgin's Son,
In bosom of thy Father's bliss.
The same to Thee, sweet Spirit be done.
As ever shall be, was and is.

The Fifth Glorious Mystery
THE CORONATION OF MARY

Blessed Virgin Mary,
you gave birth to the King of the universe
and reign with him
in the glory of heaven!

"Whoever humbles himself will be exalted!"[1] By faithfully living out these words of Jesus, his mother Mary is crowned Queen in the glory of heaven! "No servant is greater than his master"[2]: this servant of the Lord followed the sole Master, her Son. Through obedience, he emptied himself, deigning to take our mortal condition. And God raised him to his right hand "and bestowed on him the name that is above every name."[3] The humble servant Mary also fulfilled the will of the Father, and he exalted her above all the angels, to the very heights of heaven.

From now on, all ages call blessed[4] the young girl whose response to God is pure "yes": "Behold, I am the handmaid of the Lord. May it be done to me according to your word."[5] She sees her Son reign not only on the throne of David,[6] but over the entire universe. Just as she consented to be a servant, she also consents to the honor of Queen, through fidelity to the love of God.

The Mighty One has done great things for her![7] As we behold Mary crowned by her Son, it is the glory of the Church to come that we contemplate. This means that, like Mary, each one of us, as a member of the Body of Christ, is called to share in the glory of the kingdom of Christ Jesus for ever and ever!

In contemplating God's works that begin in the obscurity of Nazareth and come to fruition in the splendor of heaven, let us be guided by Mary, our Mother and our Queen. We wish to live and die in the hope of communion in her glory for all eternity.

1- Mt 23:12   2- Jn 15:20   3- Phil 2:9
4- Lk 1:48   5- Lk 1:38-43   6- Lk 1:33   7- Lk 1:49

Prayer

God of all goodness,
you willed that the mother of your Son
should be our Mother and our Queen.
With the help of her intercession,
may we one day attain heaven
and the glory promised to all your children.
Through Christ our Lord.

The Assumption of the Virgin (detail, early 16th century)
Ambrogio di Stefano da Fossano, called Bergognone (c. 1453-1523)
Oil and gold on wood, 95.25 x 42.5 in.

Numerous churches of Lombardy are adorned with altarpieces and frescoes painted by Bergognone. This Assumption of the Virgin dates from the beginning of the sixteenth century. It is the central panel in ogival form of a large polyptych. Mary is raised to heaven by eight cherubim clothed in yellow, the color of incorruptibility. Arranged like flowers on an espalier, angel musicians render homage to the new Eve as two herald angels robed in white sound the trumpets of the resurrection. Above, like a seraphic garland, a celestial choir sings praises to the Mother of God. Even as she rises upward in her glorious Assumption, Mary receives her royal crown from two angels acting on behalf of her divine Son. With open arms, he prepares to welcome her into the highest heaven. The Lord shines out in the center of a semicircle of the ranked celestial hierarchy. Angels, archangels, principalities, powers, virtues, dominions, thrones, cherubim, seraphim, all the wonderful panoply of celestial spirits is there to pay allegiance to their Queen. What joy to see our sister in humanity reigning above the angels! In contemplating her triumph, our Christian hope is rekindled, for we too, through baptism, have been promised a share in Christ's kingship. Though perhaps on a different scale, we may see in this lovely painting by Bergognone an image of the manner in which we will be received in heaven after our death. Thus in the trials and anguish of this life, sursum corda! lift up your hearts! for so says the Alpha and the Omega, who once died and now lives: "Remain faithful until death, and I will give you the crown of life" (Rv 2:8, 11).

The Battle of Lepanto (1572)
*Paolo Caliari, called Veronese (1528-1588)
Oil on canvas, 66.5 x 54 in.*

*This work painted by Veronese in
1572, one year after the event, was
commissioned by the Venetian Senate,
which had the following dedication
appended at the bottom: "Neither valor,
nor arms, nor leaders, but the rosary
of our Lady gave the victory." As the
battle rages below at sea, in the heavens
the Serenissima (Venice), symbolically
represented as a woman humbly veiled in
white, urgently begs the intercession of
Our Lady of the Rosary. She is presented
to the Virgin and supported in her appeal
by the great saints honored in the Most
Serene Republic: Saint Peter, Saint Roch
(or Rocco), Saint Justine, and Saint Mark
with a lion at his feet.*

OUR LADY
OF THE
ROSARY

In the mid-sixteenth century, the Ottoman Empire and its allies had carried Islamic power to the doors of Rome, Venice, and Vienna. The latter, besieged by more than a hundred thousand troops, had only just been saved. But Bulgaria, Serbia, Bosnia, Croatia, a large part of Greece, Hungary, Moldavia, Romania, and Albania had already been conquered. Italy was like a ripe fruit ready for the picking by Selim II, the successor to Suleiman the Magnificent. He mustered a formidable fleet off Lepanto, in the Gulf of Patras (Corinth), to deliver the *coup de grâce*. In panic, the Dominican Pope Pius V founded the Holy League, a coalition of Christian fleets, principally from Venice and Spain, under the sole command of Don John of Austria, who at the time was just twenty-four years of age. This young man, the half-brother of the emperor, Philip II, was to prove himself an admiral of genius.

THE GREATEST NAVAL BATTLE OF ALL TIME

Conscious of the desperate nature of this undertaking, the pope beseeched all Christians to pray for this Armada by a daily recitation of the rosary. The decisive battle took place on October 7, 1571. More than one hundred and fifty thousand men and at least five hundred ships gathered for the fight. It was the greatest naval battle of all time. The outcome long hung in the balance, until the confrontation finally ended in the destruction of the Muslim fleet.

Pope Pius V experienced a miraculous revelation of the victory at the same moment it was taking place. This saintly pope always maintained that the victory of Lepanto was due to the special intercession of the Virgin Mary, obtained by the praying of the rosary. In commemoration of the victory, he had the invocation *Auxilium Christianorum*, "Help of Christians," added to the Litanies of Loreto, and he established October 7 as the Feast of Our Lady of Victory. His successor, Gregory XIII, moved the feast to the first Sunday in October, celebrated henceforth as the Solemnity of the Most Holy Rosary of Our Blessed Lady. Ever since then, this feast has been especially honored whenever Christianity has come under threat. Thus it was extended to the entire Latin rite Church in 1716 by Clement XII to commemorate and encourage the liberation of Eastern Europe from the Islamic yoke. In a desire to re-establish the dominical liturgy solely as the day of the Resurrection, in 1913 Saint Pius X moved the feast day back to October 7. Twenty-four years later, in 1937, Pope Pius XI published, one after another, three resounding encyclicals. Having firmly condemned Nazism in *Mit brennender Sorge* (March 14) and Communism in *Divini Redemptoris* (March 19), he then published his testament: *Ingravescentibus malis* (September 29). To convey the grave danger which totalitarian and atheistic regimes posed to peace, the pope here reflected in detail upon the victory of Lepanto, encouraging the celebration of the feast of October 7, and he called upon the universal Church to pray the rosary.

THE VICTORY OF THE PRINCE OF PEACE

In these early years of the twenty-first century, when it is the Christian individual himself who is threatened with annihilation through the combined effects of relativism and worldly pleasures, the Church continues to guide us to devotion of Our Lady of the Rosary as the *help of Christians* who wish to live and die as disciples of Jesus Christ. But, in the end, if the Church, *Mater et Magistra*, "Mother and Teacher," invites us in the liturgy to celebrate a victory of yesteryear, it is above all to guide us toward the eternal victory—the

only victory that counts—that of the Resurrection of Christ. In the Collect of the Mass of Our Lady of the Rosary, as Pope Paul VI renamed this feast, we still pray to this day:

Pour forth, we beseech you, O Lord,
your grace into our hearts,
that we, to whom the Incarnation
of Christ your Son
was made known by the message
of an Angel,
may, through the intercession
of the Blessed Virgin Mary,
by his Passion and Cross
be brought to the glory
of his Resurrection.

By encouraging us through praying the rosary to meditate upon the mysteries of Christ with his mother Mary, the Church calls upon us to fight the good fight—that of an active faith of love—that we may be given eternal communion in the victory of the Prince of Peace. ■

Pierre-Marie Dumont

Art Credits

Front Cover: *The Annunciation* (1828), Johann von Schraudolph (1808-1879), oil on wood, Kunstmuseum, Basel, Switzerland. © Artothek / La Collection.

Page 8-9: *John Paul II's monument in Września, Poland*, marble sculpture by Iwona Jesiotr-Krupińska. © Bogdan Konopka.

Page 10: *Virgin with Child*, called *Notre-Dame-de-la-Bonne* (detail, 14th century), polychrome stone, Basilica of Saint-Quentin, France. © Jean-Paul Dumontier / La Collection.

Page 11: *Lily* (1683), from the *History of Louis le Grand*, folio 54, Jean Donneau de Visé (1638-1710), National Library of France, Paris. © BnF.

Page 12-13: *Pilgrims Entering Bethlehem on Christmas Day* (c. 1875), Félix Bonfils (1831-1885). © adoc-photos.

Page 14: *White Lily*, anonymous, National Museum of Natural History, Paris, France. © Muséum national d'Histoire naturelle, dist. RMN-GP / image du MNHN, bibliothèque centrale.

Page 15: *The Annunciation*, illumination from the *Great Hours of Anne of Brittany*, folio 26v, Jean Bourdichon (c. 1457-1521), National Library of France, Paris. © BnF.

Page 17: *The Virgin of the Annunciation* (after 1440), Altarpiece of the Magi, reverse side, left wing panel, Stephan Lochner (c. 1410-1451), oil on wood, Cologne Cathedral, Germany. © Artothek / La Collection.

Page 18: *Bouquet*, Pierre-Joseph Redouté (1759-1840), National Library of France, Paris. © BnF.

Page 19: *The Visitation*, illumination from the *Great Hours of Anne of Brittany*, folio 36v, Jean Bourdichon (c. 1457-1521), National Library of France, Paris. © BnF.

Page 21: *The Visitation* (c. 1610/1614), Domenikos Theotokopoulos, called El Greco (1541-1614), oil on canvas, Dumbarton Oaks Museum, Washington DC, USA. © DeAgostini / Leemage

Page 22: *Bouquet*, Pierre-Joseph Redouté (1759-1840), National Library of France, Paris. © BnF.

Page 23: *The Nativity*, illumination from the *Great Hours of Anne of Brittany*, folio 51v, Jean Bourdichon (c. 1457-1521), National Library of France, Paris. © BnF.

Page 25: *The Nativity*, panel from the Sant'Agostino polyptych, Pietro di Cristoforo Vannucci, called Perugino (c. 1448-1523), oil on wood, National Gallery, Perugia, Italy. © 2012, Photo Scala, Florence – courtesy of the Ministero Beni e Att. Culturali.

Page 26: *Bouquet* (1852), Pierre Anglade (19th century), National Library of France, Paris. © BnF.

Page 27: *The Presentation of Jesus in the Temple*, illumination from the *Great Hours of Anne of Brittany*, folio 70v, Jean Bourdichon (c. 1457-1521), National Library of France, Paris. © BnF.

Page 29: *The Presentation of Jesus in the Temple* (1510), Vittore Carpaccio (c. 1460-c. 1525), oil on wood, Galleria dell'Accademia, Venice, Italy. © 2012, Photo Scala, Florence – courtesy of the Ministero Beni e Att. Culturali.

Page 30: *Bouquet* (1805), Jean-Louis Prévost (c. 1760-1810), National Library of France, Paris. © BnF.

Page 31: *The Finding of Jesus in the Temple*, illumination from the *Speculum historiale* by Vincent of Beauvais, folio 206v, Master François (15th century), National Library of France, Paris. © BnF.

Page 33: *Christ among the Doctors*, Spanish School, Catalonia (15th century), tempera and gold leaf on wood, The Metropolitan Museum of Art, NYC, NY, USA. © The Metropolitan Museum of Art, Dist. RMN-GP / image of the MMA.

Page 34: *Virgin* (c. 1410), polychrome stone, National Gallery, Ljubljana, Slovenia. © Collection Dagli Orti / Galerie nationale, Ljubljana, Slovenia / Gianni Dagli Orti.

Page 35: *Sunflower* (1683), from the *History of Louis le Grand*, folio 30, Jean Donneau de Visé (1638-1710), National Library of France, Paris. © BnF.

Page 36-37: *The Jordan Issuing from Lake Tiberias* (c. 1880), Félix Bonfils (1831-1885). © adoc-photos.

Page 38: *Bouquet*, Nicolas Robert (1614-1685), National Museum of Natural History, Paris, France. © Muséum national d'Histoire naturelle, dist. RMN-GP / image du MNHN, bibliothèque centrale.

Page 39: *The Baptism of the Lord*, illumination from the *Very Rich Hours of the Duke of Berry*, Ms. 65, folio 109v, Jean Colombe (c. 1430-c. 1498), Conde Museum, Chantilly, France. © RMN-GP (Domaine de Chantilly) / René-Gabriel Ojéda.

Page 41: *The Baptism of the Lord* (1561), Paolo Caliari, called Veronese (1528-1588), Church of the Redeemer, Venice, Italy. © Luisa Ricciarini / Leemage.

Page 42: *Bouquet*, Pierre-Joseph Redouté (1759-1840), Louvre Museum, Paris, France. © RMN-GP (musée du Louvre) / Michèle Bellot.

Page 43: *The Wedding at Cana* (1460), illumination from the *Book of Hours of Amédée de Saluces* (15th century), British Library, London, United Kingdom. © akg-images / British Library.

Page 45: *The Wedding at Cana*, (13th century), stained glass, Cathedral of Notre-Dame, Chartres, France. © Jean-Paul Dumontier / La Collection.

Page 46: *Bouquet* (1805), Jean-Louis Prévost (c. 1760-1810), National Library of France, Paris. © BnF.

Page 47: *Christ Preaching*, illumination from the *Book of Hours of Louis de Laval*, folio 265, Jean Colombe (c. 1430-c. 1498), National Library of France, Paris. © BnF.

Page 49: *Christ Calling Andrew and Simon Peter* (detail, 14th century), fresco, Church of Saint John the Baptist, Origne, France. © Jean-Paul Dumontier / La Collection.

Page 50: *Bouquet*, Louis Barthélemy Fréret (1755-1831), National Library of France, Paris. © BnF.

Page 51: *The Transfiguration of the Lord*, illumination from the *Breviary of King René II of Lorraine*, Jean Bourdichon (workshop of) (c. 1457-1521), Petit-Palais Museum, Paris, France. © RMN-GP / Agence Bulloz.

Page 53: *The Transfiguration of the Lord* (c. 1594/1595), Ludovico Carracci (1555-1619), oil on wood, Pinacoteca Nazionale, Bologna, Italy. © Alinari / The Bridgeman Art Library.

Page 54: *Bouquet* (1805), Jean-Louis Prévost (c. 1760-1810), National Library of France, Paris. © BnF.

Page 55: *The Washing of the Feet*, illumination from the *Book of Hours of the use of Troyes*, ms. 3901, folio 194v, Jean Colombe (c. 1430-c. 1498), Médiathèque du Grand Troyes, France. © Photo Médiathèque du Grand Troyes.

Page 57: *The Institution of the Eucharist* (detail, 1451/1453), cell 35 in the Convent of San Marco, Fra Angelico (c. 1387-1455), fresco, San Marco Museum, Florence, Italy. © 2012, Photo Scala, Florence – courtesy of the Ministero Beni e Att. Culturali.

Page 58: *Pietà* (detail, c. 1400), anonymous German master, Bayerisches Nationalmuseum, Munich, Germany. © Bayerisches Nationalmuseum.

Page 59: *Carnation* (1683), from the *History of Louis le Grand*, folio 68, Jean Donneau de Visé (1638-1710), National Library of France, Paris. © BnF.

Page 60-61: *View of the Garden of Gethsemane near Jerusalem* (c. 1853), Robertson & Beato (19th century). © Musée Nicéphore Niépce, Chalon-sur-Saône, France / adoc-photos.

Page 62: *Bouquet* (1805), Jean-Louis Prévost (c. 1760-1810), National Library of France, Paris. © BnF.

Page 63: *The Agony in the Garden*, illumination from the *Book of Hours of Louis de Laval*, folio 94, Jean Colombe (c. 1430-c. 1498), National Library of France, Paris. © BnF.

Page 65: *Christ on the Mount of Olives* (1819), Francisco José de Goya y Lucientes (1746-1828), oil on wood, Colegio Escolapios de San Antón, Madrid, Spain. © akg-images / Erich Lessing.

Page 66: *Bouquet*, Pierre-Joseph Redouté (1759-1840), National Library of France, Paris. © BnF.

Page 67: *The Scourging at the Pillar* (c. 1515), illumination from the *Da Costa Hours*, ms. M.399, folio 44v, Pierpont Morgan Library, NYC, NY, USA. © 2012, Photo Pierpont Morgan Library / art Resource / Scala, Florence.

Page 69: *Christ Bound to the Column*, Alonso Cano (1601-1667), oil on canvas, Museum of Fine Arts, Pau, France. © Musée des Beaux-Arts de Pau / Jean-Christophe Poumeyrol.

Page 70: *Bouquet* (1852), Pierre Anglade (19th century), National Library of France, Paris. © BnF.

Page 71: *The Crowning with Thorns* (c. 1515), illumination from the *Da Costa Hours*, ms. M.399, folio 58v, Pierpont Morgan Library, NYC, NY, USA. © 2012, Photo Pierpont Morgan Library / art Resource / Scala, Florence.

Page 73: *The Crowning with Thorns* (c. 1510), detail of the Passion Altarpiece, Champagne or Picardy workshop, polychrome limestone, Chapel of Notre-Dame de la Houssaye, Pontivy, France. © Clément Guillaume.

Page 74: *Bouquet*, Pierre-Joseph Redouté (1759-1840), National Library of France, Paris. © BnF.

Page 75: *Christ Carrying the Cross*, illumination from the *Book of Hours of the use of Tours*, Harley 2877, folio 44v, Jean Bourdichon (c. 1457-1521), The British Library, London, England. © Heritage Images / Leemage.

Page 77: *Christ and the Cyrenian* (detail, 1547), Tiziano Vecellio di Gregorio, called Titian (c. 1488-1576), oil on canvas, Prado Museum, Madrid, Spain. © 2012, Photo Scala, Florence.

Page 78: *Bouquet*, Pierre-Joseph Redouté (1759-1840), National Library of France, Paris. © BnF.

Page 79: *The Crucifixion*, illumination from the *Great Hours of Anne of Brittany*, folio 47v, Jean Bourdichon (c. 1457-1521), National Library of France, Paris. © BnF.

Page 81: *The Crucifixion* (1392-1393), Piero di Giovanni, called Lorenzo Monaco (c. 1370-c. 1424), tempera and gilding on wood, Accademia Gallery, Florence, Italy. © 2012, Photo Scala, Florence – courtesy of the Ministero Beni e Att. Culturali.

Page 82: *The Virgin Mary at Prayer* (detail, before 1412), polychrome wood, Church of Santa Maria della Libera, Cercemaggiore, Italy. © akg-images / Electa.

Page 83: *The Rose* (1683), from the *History of Louis le Grand*, folio 58, Jean Donneau de Visé (1638-1710), National Library of France, Paris. © BnF.

Page 84-85: *Tomb of Saint James in Jerusalem* (beginning of 19th century), Jacques Boyer. © Jacques Boyer / Roger-Viollet.

Page 86: *Bouquet*, Pierre-Joseph Redouté (1759-1840), National Library of France, Paris. © BnF.

Page 87: *The Resurrection*, illumination from the *Very Rich Hours of the Duke of Berry*, ms. 65, folio 182r, Jean Colombe (c. 1430-c. 1498), Conde Museum, Chantilly, France. © RMN-GP (Domaine de Chantilly) / René-Gabriel Ojéda.

Page 89: *The Resurrection* (detail, c. 1570), Paolo Caliari, called Veronese (1528-1588), oil on canvas, Gemäldegalerie Alte Meister, Dresden, Germany. © BPK, Berlin, dist. RMN / Elke Estel / Hans-Peter Kluth.

Page 90: *Bouquet*, Pierre-Joseph Redouté (1759-1840), National Library of France, Paris. © BnF.

Page 91: *The Ascension*, illumination from the *Book of Hours of Etienne Chevalier*, ms. 71, folio 3r, Jean Fouquet (1420-c. 1477), Conde Museum, Chantilly, France. © RMN-GP (Domaine de Chantilly) / René-Gabriel Ojéda.

Page 93: *The Ascension* (c. 1460/1464), Andrea Mantegna (1431-1506), tempera on wood, Uffizi Gallery, Florence, Italy. © 2012, Photo Scala, Florence – courtesy of the Ministero Beni e Att. Culturali.

Page 94: *Bouquet*, P. Lambotte (19th century), National Library of France, Paris. © BnF.

Page 95: *The Descent of the Holy Spirit*, illumination from the *Great Hours of Anne of Brittany*, folio 49v, Jean Bourdichon (c. 1457-1521), National Library of France, Paris. © BnF.

Page 97: *The Descent of the Holy Spirit* (1612/1613), Fray Juan Bautista Maíno (1581-1649), from the altarpiece in the Monastery of Saint Peter Martyr, Toledo, oil on canvas, Prado Museum, Madrid, Spain. © Album / Oronoz / akg.

Page 98: *Bouquet*, anonymous (19th century), National Library of France, Paris. © BnF.

Page 99: *The Assumption of the Virgin*, illumination from the *Book of Hours of Etienne Chevalier*, ms. 71, folio 12, Jean Fouquet (1420-c. 1477), Conde Museum, Chantilly, France. © RMN-GP (Domaine de Chantilly) / René-Gabriel Ojéda.

Page 101: *The Death and the Assumption of the Virgin* (c. 1432), Guido di Pietro, called Fra Angelico (c. 1387-1455), tempera and gold on wood, Isabella Stewart Gardner Museum, Boston, MA, USA. © Isabella Stewart Gardner Museum, Boston, MA, USA / The Bridgeman Art Library.

Page 102: *Bouquet*, Pierre-Joseph Redouté (1759-1840), National Museum of Natural History, Paris, France. © Muséum national d'Histoire naturelle, dist. RMN-GP / image du MNHN, bibliothèque centrale.

Page 103: *The Assumption of the Virgin*, illumination from *Frederick III of Aragon's Book of Hours*, page 308, Jean Bourdichon (c. 1457-1521), National Library of France, Paris. © BnF.

Page 105: *The Assumption of the Virgin* (detail), Ambrogio di Stefano da Fossano, called Bergognone (c. 1453-1523), oil and gold on wood, Metropolitan Museum of Art, NYC, USA. © The Metropolitan Museum of Art, Dist. RMN-GP / image of the MMA.

Page 106: *The Battle of Lepanto* (1572), Paolo Caliari, called Veronese (1528-1588), oil on canvas, Gallerie dell'Accademia, Venice, Italy. © 2012, Photo Scala, Florence – courtesy of the Ministero Beni e Att. Culturali.

Back cover: *Virgin with the Host* (1854), Jean-Auguste-Dominique Ingres (1780-1867), oil on canvas (tondo), 44.5 in. diameter, Musée d'Orsay, Paris, France. © 2012, photo Scala, Florence.

Hymn Credits

Printed in October 2012 by Transcontinental, Canada
Edition number: MGN12012
www.magnificat.com